T0197177

First Things First

Navigating Our Challenging Times through the Words of Jesus

Jay Slife

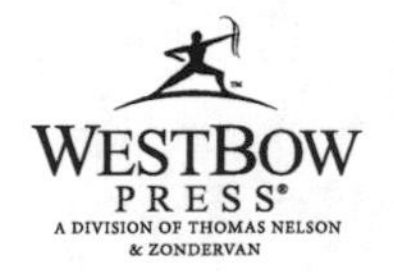

TheBuild.org
Jay@TheBuild.org

WestBow Press books may be ordered through booksellers or by contacting:

WestBow Press
A Division of Thomas Nelson & Zondervan
1663 Liberty Drive
Bloomington, IN 47403
www.westbowpress.com
1 (866) 928-1240

ISBN: 978-1-9736-6523-6 (sc)
ISBN: 978-1-9736-6524-3 (hc)
ISBN: 978-1-9736-6525-0 (e)

Library of Congress Control Number: 2019943860

Print information available on the last page.

WestBow Press rev. date 07/15/2019

Dedication

This book is dedicated to my wife, Julia, who is my lifelong soul mate, my best friend, my confidant, mine to the end. She is the one who stood by my side through it all, never giving up, always encouraging me. She is the one with whom I have learned life. She is the one my heavenly Father used to demonstrate to me, over and over until I got it, the tangible reality of unconditional love. Thank you, my dear and precious wife, for all that you are.

Contents

Introduction

A Word for You

It has been my experience, in sixty-plus years of living and thirty-eight-plus years in the realm of Christian ministry, that many who believe in and call on the name of Jesus are so beat up, so beat down, or so guilt or shame driven for any number of reasons, some self-inflicted and some not, that they see God and his Word negatively. They see it from a vantage point wherein his communiqués are "just another thing I can't live up to." Or, "His Word just does not add up for me and my life experience."

For many, this place is where they live, it is how they feel, it is their experience, and it is understood in all its difficulty. Perhaps this is the case for you. The sense and personal reality of this *seems* true; it *feels* true. Jesus has a different understanding; he sees a bigger picture.

I am choosing to start this adventure with something that offers what *is* true, perhaps to be seen from a different perspective, perhaps to be seen for the first time:

Ephesians chapter 1 is an absolute diamond mine regarding what is true about who and what you are, whether or not you see it, agree with it, understand it, or accept it. Let's look at a few of the diamonds:

In verse 1 it says, "Paul, an apostle of Christ Jesus by the *will* of God, to the *saints* in Ephesus, the *faithful* in Christ Jesus" (emphasis mine).

You are the want of God

Paul states, and is operating in, the will of God. If you are born again and actively working at walking with Jesus, you also are operating in the will of God probably more than you realize, and perhaps more than you are giving yourself credit for. The Greek word used here translates into English as *will*, the will of God. It can also be translated as *want*, as it is in some other places in the New Testament. It is the will of God; it is also the want of God.[1] Thus, it is fair and accurate to say and understand that you are the want of God. He wants you. In whatever state or condition you currently reside. In your state of uncertainty, confusion, unconfessed or ongoing sin, fear, bondage, struggle, or misery, he wants you. In your state of bliss, joy, fulfillment, confidence, and victory, he wants you. And anywhere in between you may find yourself, he wants you.

You are part of the faithful in God

We are all in the process of development. Theologically it is called sanctification. Practically it is called character development. None of us has arrived; none of us will on this side of glory. It is not about arriving; it is all about the process, the journey. If you are actively seeking and pursuing personal relationship with Jesus, you are part of the faithful in God. This is true regardless of how it might seem, feel, or look. You and your perspectives are not the unit of measure here; his are. (More on this later.) A case in point would be Abraham, who is called the father of the faith, who was called righteous.[2] And yet he stumbled. He lied, he failed, he covered up and manipulated. He made and accumulated many mistakes, some quite course-changing and historical. So why is he then called and counted as righteous? Because he was faithful. Because he recognized, and lived, in the faithfulness of his God. Because despite all the circumstances and situations that stood in front of him, many of which were simply beyond his control, he trusted that Yahweh was who he said he was and would do what he said he would do. He could be trusted. If you know Jesus, then in your heart of hearts you know that to be true. That makes you part of the faithful in God.

You are an awful thing!

The word *saint* is accurately and most often defined as "set apart" or "sacred." It means to be physically pure, morally blameless, and even ceremonially consecrated. If you are born again, then in, by, and through the blood of Jesus this is who you are.

But check it out: the base meaning of *saint* is "awful thing."[3] That is Old English spelling. In today's world, it would be spelled "awe-full thing." It means "one inspiring awe." It means "highly impressive." The Lord, the Creator of the Universe, is here saying that you cause him to be full of awe. He is in awe of and over you! Awe means "a sense of reverence and wonder inspired by the greatness or superiority of a person; so inspiring as to bring on an immobilizing effect."[4] That is what the Lord Most High thinks of you! According to him:

> You are awful!
>
> You inspire awe in God!
>
> You bring a sense of wonder to him by your very being!
>
> You bring an immobilizing effect upon him!
>
> You are so grand as to stop him in his tracks!
>
> You take his breath away!
>
> You are awe-full!

Now, that's the *truth* about you!

In verses 17–19 it says,

> …that the God of our Lord Jesus Christ, the glorious Father, may *give* you the Spirit of *wisdom* and *revelation*, so that you may know him better, … that the eyes of your *heart* may be *enlightened* in order that you may know the *hope* to which he has called you, the *riches* of his glorious *inheritance* in the saints [the awful things], and his incomparably great *power* for us who believe. (emphasis mine)

You are to be the receptor of his hope, richness, and power

Jesus wants to give you his wisdom, his revelation. He wants to open your heart to that place where you can see and know his heart. He wants to do this for you so that you can fully embrace the hope he has for you, the richness of his inheritance, which is you. You are his inheritance, and his glory, power, and presence. He wants all of this not only for you but with you! Again, that's the truth about you, and that's good news!

To Be Noted

- I am operating under the assumption that the following is true. Hebrews 4:12 says, "For the Word of God is living and active and sharper than any two-edged sword, and piercing as far as the division of soul and spirit, of both joints and marrow, and able to judge the thoughts and intentions of the heart." The word *judge* in this place is not as it may seem. It is not to judge things or people. It is to weigh and measure for the purpose of help, growth, and fulfillment. Thus, the word is not for the purpose of judgment as much as for encouragement, edification, direction, and help for us. Within the same context, four verses later it says, "Let us therefore draw near with confidence to the throne of grace, that we may receive mercy and may find grace to help in time of need." The Word is the standard for all of life. It truly is the operator's manual for all of life! It has been said that when all else fails, read the owner's manual. I choose to study in and live by the Manual before all else fails!

- I bring English, Greek, and Hebrew grammar, word study, and literary tools to the table for several reasons. One is that language morphs over time, which means that definitions, meanings, nuances, and understandings often morph as well.

The Word itself does not morph, but the words therein, when bringing them forward into the current day, can bring some confusion. It is always best and most accurate to return to the manuscripts, the writings that are as close to the original as possible. This leaves less room for error. Some interpretations are wonderful, very close, and accurate; some not so much. To get to the original languages and writings is to get to the original meanings, nuances, implications, and the like.

- These elements of language are like numbers. Numbers do not lie; they are just numbers. Although they can be manipulated to say whatever one wishes, as they stand, they don't lie. These elements are the same. When allowed to stand on their own without manipulation, misreading, or misapplication, the fullest meaning and thus application will come forth. Any language is a complex beast! It must be respected as it stands and understood from that place. The true position regarding the Word of God is then seen. I have the choice: stand in my own understanding, which truly is based on the human issues of fear, pride, and rebellion, and adjust the Word to me—or walk in brokenness and humility and allow the Word to adjust me to him (John 1).

- There is an assumption within the previous paragraph. When we get to the fullest meaning of the words, the text, we then get to the fullest possible application. This presumes that behind our pursuit of the Word is Holy Spirit working the fullness of him, of his Word into us. This then assumes two things. One, we are not driving the text for our own purposes. This is called proof-texting, which is man leading the Word to his conclusions for his gain. It is unfortunately all too common. Two, we are allowing the Author to lead, to have his way, to work his truth from his Word into our hearts and minds, into our lives. This is Lordship, his and distinctly not ours.

- There are times when I refer to the Septuagint. It is a Greek rendering of the Old Testament, which is almost entirely Hebrew. The Septuagint was the Bible of preference for good reason for over six hundred years. It was translated by Hebrew men who were also scholars but lived in a world where Greek was the common language of the day, and so it is highly respected as perhaps the most accurate and exact Hebrew-to-Greek translation of the Old Testament.

- On several occasions throughout this book, I interject the word [Selah]. This word comes from the Psalms. It is probably a musical term because many of the Psalms are actually songs. It most often means to pause, to rest, to stop, and even to meditate or consider. Here, it is intended to encourage the reader to take a pause and let the thought or idea you've just read catch up to you. Then think and meditate about it and allow the Lord to speak to you. He has much more to say, at much higher value, than I do.

- I use the word *man* in two different manners. There are times when I use it as man, the male species, and there are also times when I use it as man, humankind, which includes men, women, and children. I am not differentiating in the text, but the context should make it clear.

- A hint for easier reading: There are quite a few quotes and points of reference throughout this book. This is for those who want to follow up with their own research. They are there for you if you want. If not, ignore them and simply read right through them. Your reading experience will be much smoother that way.

Chapter 1

First Things

I am studying and writing on the Beatitudes for several reasons. First and foremost, I am responding to a prompt from my Lord and King, who has stirred and challenged me repeatedly to do this. This stirring has been building in my heart for some time and has become quite strong. Now it is time, his and mine, to accomplish this assignment. The timing clearly has somewhat to do with the time in which we live, the increasing anger and hatred in our land, and all of its subsequent actions: The sometimes overwhelming fear in the hearts of so many, and the certainly overwhelming need for the One who can save us from all this, from ourselves.

Another reason for writing this is that in my opinion, in current times very little has been offered on this portion of Scripture that actually hits the mark. There has been much by way of intelligentsia, with its assumed and inbred societal and humanistic application, much by means of interpolation (which is basically to interject into the original languages with another, laying it over the original and thus altering it, and then bringing that into English) but very little through spiritual truth, heart, and depth, followed with practical application.

The word *beatitude* comes from French, with its origins in Latin. In Latin it means "perfect" or "supreme blessedness." It has been incorrectly translated into English with a variety of words, the most common as "exalted happiness." There will be more on this later.

The Beatitudes are the beginnings of what is referred to as the Sermon on the Mount, which is the first recorded teaching of Jesus. The entire sermon is foundational to all that follows, certainly in the life and times of Jesus then, and all the more to those following him then and now. "The lifestyle which Jesus adopted for himself and called his disciples to adopt was one which exemplified the Sermon on the Mount, especially the Beatitudes."[1]

This sermon, including the Beatitudes, are key, essential, critical teachings for all of life. This is Kingdom, the essence of the Kingdom of God defined. It has been said that humble obedience to the Beatitudes is *the* condition for entering the Kingdom of God. This is Jesus cutting to the quick, laying it all out there in its fullness with no pretext or pretense for us to hear, see, understand, embrace, experience, and follow. This is not just godly parameters by which to pattern your life. This is his heart. This is his character, his personality, his person. And it all fully reflects his Father. This is what and where he wants us and is inviting and calling us to live, to live by, to live in. All of life and its experiences—up, down, good, bad, and ugly—can be, and are meant to be, lived through the person and the principles offered here. Those who choose to do so have their houses, their lives, built on the Rock. Those who don't, don't (Matthew 7:24–27).

Perhaps it might be seen this way:

Jesus has just entered into the fullness of his earthly calling. He has just become the president of a new business, if you will—the CEO of a new corporation. It is called the Kingdom of God (Daniel 7:13–14; Matthew 3:2, 4:17). As is always the case, communication is critical to the formation, the building, the advancement, and the success of any business. Thus, his first words—what he lays out, teaches, and establishes first—would be of utmost importance, of greatest value, the most significant. They would set the standard, the foundation for all that follows. The first communication from Jesus is the Sermon on the Mount, of which the Beatitudes are first! They are the first of the first, the most important of the most important!

What the Beatitudes bring to the table are revolutionary to the twenty-first century. They offer a means of living life that is totally contrary to the collective understanding, the common knowledge of the day, unfortunately even and often within Christian circles. They are totally amazing and, if embraced and followed, bring not only a new perspective but a new manner of life. But this is not some new self-help concept, some seven-step model to a new and improved you. To the contrary, this is life as created, defined, established, and intended by the Creator.

In my early years of ministry, I was given the opportunity to preach on Sunday evenings at our church. On one particular evening, after waxing eloquent on some subject I have long since forgotten, and not flowing in much mercy or grace, one of the elders of the church approached me. She and her husband were of very sweet spirit, having walked with and served Jesus for many years. They were spiritual parents for us in those days. She called me out and said something that was so amazingly profound that it flew right past me. It took me awhile to fully capture it. She said, "Jay, you need to learn something. You need to learn that God is interested in three things. He is interested in relationship. He is interested in relationship. And he is interested in relationship!"

Over time, I have come to understand the truth and value of that statement very well. All of creation, all of life, all the things he is doing and has done for and with us, and continues to do for and with us, is about relationship. All is found and founded within relationship. All of creation, all of time, all of eternity, and all of him in us and us in him is centered in relationship from and with him. He created us for relationship. We are here to worship him, an act and expression of relationship. He, his Son, and Holy Spirit are one; that is relationship. He has it in store that we become the bride of his Son, Jesus the Christ; that is relationship. Jesus came for us, died for us, and sent his Holy Spirit for us—again, all in the realm of relationship. The Pharisees asked Jesus what was the greatest commandment. His response? You guessed it: relationship. "Love the Lord your God with all your heart, mind, soul and strength," often referred to as the Great Commandment (Matthew 22:37-40; Luke 10:27). Having said that, as he often did, Jesus seized the moment of the question to teach and went on. "And the second is like it: Love your neighbor as yourself." Relationship. The word *like* in that verse is easily misunderstood. It would better come into English as "the same as" because of its mood, and thus it would read: "And the second is the same as the first." When understood in that manner, it reinforces the intensity and meaning of the Commandment. From the beginning, he created us for relationship as sons and daughters. That makes him Father, and we are to follow him and his lead. He knows best.

Does the clay say to the potter, "Why have you made me so, [and just what are you doing to me anyway?]" (Isaiah 64:8). It is called Lordship. He leads; we follow. It works best that way.

We tend to ask him to bless whatever it is that we want to do or be, that we think is best for us. He loves us and does often bless us. But quite often that settles into the good that is not the best. I don't know about you, but I want what is best, and I am willing to sacrifice the good to get it. His Lordship brings me to the place of yielding, submitting my will and my want to his. The Beatitudes spell this out. They are the road map from which we gain direction. They are the standard, the plumb line by which we are called to weigh and measure all things, by which we move forward through life according to their instruction and direction. They are the truth from which all of life flows and goes. Sound right? To some, it may sound lofty, hypothetical, and frankly impossible. But read on.

One of the realities in this walk with God that must be seen and embraced is this: The standard Jesus is here establishing, and insisting on, is not attainable in our human levels of understanding, strength, or behavior. This is by design because at the same time, in the same breath, it is fully attainable because he is right here to help. This is a spiritual principle that runs throughout Scripture, throughout life with him. One example of this principle is found in Hebrews, where it clearly states that "without faith it is impossible to please God" (Hebrews 11:6). Tall order. Then in Ephesians, it says that faith is a gift from him, with the implication to take as much as you want (Ephesians 2:8). On one hand, he states the requirement, the directive, the command. On the other hand, he gives us what we need to fulfill that command. What a wonderful transaction for us! In him, this principle runs true across the board. It is true in the context of the Beatitudes as well. That to which he is calling us comes with his help and provision to accomplish. It is relationship.

It is covenant. Several times in the Old Testament, we find Father, Yahweh, establishing covenant with his people (Genesis 15:9–21). The parameters are so amazingly wonderful for us, the receptors of his actions. He is the activist, the initiator, the establisher, the pursuer. And then if covenant is broken, he is even the receptor of negative consequence, all within said covenant![2] The Beatitudes are New Testament covenant. Then and now, this is full demonstration of his unconditional love and care for us, while in the same vein establishing his Lordship. When we choose to follow, to yield our selves and our agendas, our desires, intentions, goals, and actions to him, he becomes Lord. (He is Lord whether we choose to receive it or not. When we make these choices, he becomes the Lord of our lives.) And we live life to the full, in freedom and peace, in contentment and fulfillment, covered and protected by the One who controls it all.

His Lordship over us puts us in the position of servants to him. For many, that statement can raise the hairs on the back of their neck. Pride runs deep in the human soul! "Who is he to tell me what to do?" The upside of that assertion is the true and full freedom found therein. All his; all by design. If Jesus is my Lord, that means he is my Overseer, which ultimately means it is he who carries the responsibility for me. We brought four children into this world. Although at this point they are all grown and gone, for many years they were fully and totally our responsibility. Even now, we share deep relationship with them all, which occasionally brings input, counsel, and sometimes direction to their lives. That is the same as the Lord's position with us, except we are ever growing up and living under his headship. What freedom! What peace and joy are found when I first let go of me and then submit myself to him! It is the ultimate of intimacy, the ultimate of deep, rich relationship between the Creator and the created. And for this, we were created (Colossians 1:16; Revelation 4:11).

We don't live here. Often, we don't even know to live here. We truly do not know what we do not know. We have not been informed of, exposed to, encouraged, and taught how to live here. There is no condemnation in this—only an invitation, a challenge, an opportunity. From my heart, given from Father, from Son, from Holy Spirit.

Jesus said, "Cast not your pearls before swine" (Matthew 7:6). And, "The Kingdom is like a pearl of great price" (Matthew 13:46). All too often, we have not only cast our pearls, but in some measure we have become the swine. Again, there is no condemnation in this. Only a teardrop, a broken heart over the condition of us, of the Body of Christ, coupled with the resolve to shift and be changed that comes only from that same Father, that same Son, that same Holy Spirit. It is a resolve, a love, that is birthed in the truth that "I will never leave you, nor forsake you" (Hebrews 13:5). And, "Come to me, all you who are weary and burdened, and I will give you rest. Take my yoke upon you and learn from me, for I am gentle and humble in heart, and you will find rest for your souls. For my yoke is easy and my burden is light" (Matthew 11:28–30). And that says, "Stay close, son. We will work through this together."[3] No, we don't live here. We don't know to live here. But the invitation is as fresh and new and vibrant today as it was some two thousand years ago, when it was first spoken, first offered. I want that. How about you?

It needs to be seen that this writing is not an attempt, by revisiting Scripture long ago highlighted within Christian circles, to return to a time gone by, to a time when life was easier. Neither is it intended to console us so we can settle into a life with our heads in the sand, ignoring this present danger. To the contrary, this is a call—a command, even—amid some of the most challenging and difficult times in human history to step into a life that becomes a lifestyle, that will bring radical transformation into your life, your family, your community, and even your nation. This brings the Kingdom front and center, where it will impact you and all people, whether or not they know and follow Jesus.

Unfortunately, it seems the current condition of the Church, and society at large (at least in the United States) is well defined from two Scriptures. Proverbs 13:12 says, "Hope deferred makes the heart grow sick," while Proverbs 29:18 says, "Where there is no vision, the people perish" (KJV). Let's break this down a bit and then consider the second part of each of these Scriptures.

There is a tremendous amount of hope deferred in our land. Within one particular people group (millennials), it seems to be their base definition for all of life; but it is present in many others as well. Hope is deferred, is put off because of its lack, because of its absence in the day-to-day and in the ongoing difficult and painful struggles and routines of life. Unresolved conflict and unsettled issues can produce bitterness toward the people involved, toward self, and even toward God. Left unchecked, this can result in spite and stubbornness (which is really rebellion) that can carry on repeatedly for years. This is the seed, the breeding ground for hope deferred. This is very real to so many, and it seems now to be an ever-growing reality. But the second half of the verse must be captured: "but a longing fulfilled is a tree of life." This deferred hope comes from any number of sources, a longing fulfilled comes from but One. Proverbs 3:18 says, "[Wisdom] is a tree of life to those who embrace her; those who lay hold of her will be blessed." And who is the Author of wisdom? Jesus. Father God. And what does it mean to be blessed? Basically, it is to be favored and highly esteemed. (see chapter 2). Jesus is the Tree of Life (Revelation 2:7), and he brings a tree of life to all who walk with him in the manner in which he calls us to walk. Hope deferred is real and present. So is Jesus. He turns the former into the latter. He "revives and strengthens"[4] when we seek his face and live accordingly.

[Selah]

In Proverbs 29:18, the word translated as *vision* literally means a revelatory word, a divine communication, a prophecy from God that brings vision. That would be none other than the Creator of the Universe speaking to his loved creation. I'm not sure how that would fit in your world, but hearing from the Lord equates to a strong stirring of my heart, which brings a great peace and subsequent enthusiasm along with a renewed hope. The result of that is renewed or further direction from him, followed by an applicable action by me, and giving rise to a furthering sense of purpose and value. That defines the second portion of the verse: "but blessed is he who keeps [and so follows] the way of the Lord."

The word translated as *perish* means "to loosen," "to dismiss."[5] It is to be unbridled, to be undisciplined, to become lawless. The King James Version uses the word *perish* because that is the end result of this action, of this having no vision. The New International Version and the New American Standard Bible use the words *unrestrained* and *cast off restraint*, respectively. As I have studied and pressed into this passage, the Lord said to me, assured me, that the problem is not on his end. In other words, the fact that we are not receiving this revelatory communication is not that he is not speaking but that we are having a difficult time hearing or responding fully to what we are hearing. (See my website for a thorough study on hearing the voice of God.)

I could probably write a book about all the happenings in my life that have contributed to the sense of hope deferred and of little or no revelation. I imagine many could write that book. I could also probably write several books on the wonderful side of my life, especially with the Lord and my wife and family. In all honesty, it needs to be said that some of those struggles had and still have to do with the choices, attitudes, and actions in which I have chosen to walk. I recognize that some of that is far outside my ability to direct or control. Still, much of it remains as a large part of my life—and of yours too, I think. My point is that for many, life and all its circumstances and situations are more difficult and draining than they ever thought it would be or even could be.

I was in China in 2016 on a mission trip. It was wonderful. The Lord was very present and accounted for! Upon my return, I was asked repeatedly what I experienced in the hearts and lives of the local people I encountered. As I thought and pondered this question, the answer became quite clear. What I saw in the people, most of them brothers and sisters in Christ, was something I don't see much of in my country: a true hope and a hunger for the deeper things of God. I think either one breeds and gives place to the other. I am not here to talk about societal or political points of view, or to cast any blame upon anyone. I am here to acknowledge the problems, challenges, and difficulties we all face. I am also here to offer a "ways and means" to not just manage all of that but to actually live in a hope, with a hunger that results in rising above and living in the depths of great peace, fulfillment, and contentment.

I believe, and know to be true, that a walk with Jesus based on and always returning to these Beatitudes brings this fulfillment to its greatest extent. I also know this fulfillment can be gained in no other manner.

Points to attain before we proceed:

1. In order to grasp and fully embrace these Beatitudes, it must be seen and understood that they are absolutely and unequivocally designed and offered as basic foundational parts

> of life itself, for all of life. That is life as it is meant to be lived within God's Kingdom, of which we are a part and within which we are called to walk. As has already been spoken, these nine offerings form the basis for all of the teachings of Jesus that follow, and from there all of life. Any and all elements or components that comprise this life (your life and mine) are intended to come from this base.

I was once invited into a cluster of house church entities to consult, teach, and speak prophetically, should the Lord direct. Early on in this assignment, I was in one of the homes, the leader of which was a man with good intentions. As the meeting went on, Father gave me a clear prophetic word for this man and the work he was doing within his group: green concrete. This was a difficult word to deliver—and no doubt an even more difficult word to hear. Green concrete is not that which comes out of the truck green in color. Green concrete is concrete that, although it looks and flows like normal concrete when wet, for one of several reasons is not properly mixed and so does not properly cure. The net result is concrete that looks normal but has little or no structural integrity. After it sets, when it is subjected to the weight and pressure that comes from what is built upon it, it crumbles and fails. The subsequent result can be disastrous because all may well come tumbling down, not always immediately but over time.

The challenge is to recognize the "greenness" before it is put into service. You can see the ramifications of this when brought into a leadership role, or really anywhere in one's life. If the foundation upon which one is building and basing one's life experience is cemented in green concrete, it will not hold up and stand strong when exposed to weight and pressure. Although this man's intentions were good, his lack of character, inner strength, and ability to healthily withstand life's pressures were adversely affecting him, his wife and family, and his ministry. It was evident. A close, prophetic look into his marriage and family revealed large cracks. Those who were following his lead were really struggling. I am not sharing this story to bring shame or condemnation to this man but to illustrate what readily happens to any of us who has built, or is building, a life not based on the truth and standards of the Word. This contrast is nowhere more evidenced than within these Beatitudes. Built here, life will take on the full intent of Father when he created it all. Built on some other base or foundation, it will be green concrete and will crack and crumble—and most often come to some very difficult, even disastrous conclusion.

2. The Beatitudes are the attributes of the King. They are the character traits, the personality, of Jesus. The key to the whole of this message is found in Matthew 5:11: "on account of me" (NASB). This phrase certainly finds its meaning within its immediate context. It also finds a broader meaning within the larger content of the entirety of the Beatitudes. All of this is on, and in, and about him. The very life, the very heart, of the Lord Jesus is herein to be discovered and put into place and practice. These are the strategies for life, direct from the King to you. What a way to live! As such, they are only truly seen and embraced through the insights and perspectives of the Kingdom, his Kingdom—not the world, not the natural way.

Allow me to take that statement further. The strategies needed to build a life with right standing and right relationships, such as a marriage and family, must come from these Beatitudes and the principles and practices they bring. This statement is also true regarding any career path or business, any church or ministry, any expression of the Great Commandment or the Great Commission that engages the lives of others.

3. From my understanding and perspective, in the exact context within which they are presented, the Beatitudes are progressive, each building on the preceding one in the genius that can only come from the Author. They are like concrete blocks used in the construction of a wall or the foundation of a building. Though they can each stand alone, when placed together there is a unity, even a community, among them. As they are placed together, they gain in strength, the sum being more than the total of the parts. They are truly synergistic. It is nothing less than sheer brilliance, the manner in which the Author has designed and constructed all of his Word. That is no more evident than within this section of Scripture. The first four weave and build an amazing spiritual reality, clearly reflecting the character of Jesus, working together to create a phenomenal base. One could stop, absorb, and apply just there and be well set for the rest of one's life. There is a corner turned after that, the base having been built. The four together now move into the following five singularly, extending that base, establishing truth in each sphere of expression. It seems formed as such: one to two; one and two to three; and one, two and three to four. Then it becomes one through four to five, and then to six, and on. Go figure: the Creator is very creative!

4. It is to be noted that these Beatitudes, these blessings, are not offered or to be seen with a "sense of consolation." "To the contrary, they offer a present and a future that are a radical alteration of what was [or what is without them]."[6] Said another way, they are not intended to console, which might be derived by the repeated use of the word *bless* and its current understanding, but rather to stir and challenge one into a radical way of life, which they fully define. Radical here would be a position mostly opposite of the place where modern, mainstream Christianity finds itself. I think that for

fear of being labeled as fanatical in our culture, and pressured by political correctness, many have given up on the call to be radical. Jesus certainly was not fanatical. He certainly was radical. And over and over he is our example and calls us to follow his lead (Philippians 2:5–8).

5. I am looking at these Beatitudes in a current time frame. Many have them in a future setting. Historically, they have been seen primarily with an eschatological understanding, speaking to the future, to eternity. Although this is true, they carry a very strong message for today that is ever stronger as we come more and more into the increases of national and global conflict. George Eldon Ladd said it this way: "I feel [the Beatitudes] as well, *and perhaps of most import*, teach a present blessedness" (emphasis mine).[7] It's a present blessedness, a present worldview and subsequent lifestyle that must be fully in place for what is to come. If we will walk with him through this current and coming struggle, we must be living here.

Here is my prayer for you as you go on.

In Matthew 5:1–2, as Jesus was setting up to offer the Sermon, the Beatitudes, "his disciples came to him and he began to teach them." The word *disciple* is not a casual word. A disciple is a determined learner. To be discipled would be to be determinedly learned or taught. A disciple-er would be one who teaches in a very decided or resolved manner. In this way, Jesus taught and they learned. Clearly it is not that they merely listened. No, they were determined learners, tenacious learners. They were Hebrews who knew from their Hebraic way of life that to listen, to hear, and so to learn was to apply. They were willing, even eager, to learn by way of understanding but also by way of action and experience, through application, bringing full, deep purpose into life. That is exactly what we all are called to. Be a disciple. Be a doer of the Word, not just a hearer (James 1:22, 2:14–24). Then be a disciple-er. Hear it. Learn it. Live it. Then give it away by, in, and for the name of Jesus.

The Text: Matthew 5:3–16

3. Blessed are the poor in spirit, for theirs is the kingdom of heaven.

4. Blessed are those who mourn, for they will be comforted.

5. Blessed are the meek, for they will inherit the earth.

6. Blessed are those who hunger and thirst for righteousness, for they will be filled.

7. Blessed are the merciful, for they will be shown mercy.

8. Blessed are the pure in heart, for they will see God.

9. Blessed are the peacemakers, for they will be called sons of God.

10. Blessed are those who are persecuted because of righteousness, for theirs is the kingdom of heaven.

11. Blessed are you when people insult you, persecute you, and falsely say all kinds of evil against you because of me.

12. Rejoice and be glad, because great is your reward in heaven, for in the same way they persecuted the prophets who were before you.

13. You are the salt of the earth. But if the salt loses its saltiness, how can it be made salty again? It is no longer good for anything, except to be thrown out and trampled by men.

14. You are the light of the world. A city on a hill cannot be hidden.

15. Neither do people light a lamp and put it under a bowl. Instead they put it on its stand, and it gives light to everyone in the house.

16. In the same way let you light shine before men, that they may see your good deeds and praise your Father in heaven.

Although the Beatitudes formally end after verse 12, there is a direct connection with them and the next four verses—thus their inclusion here.

Chapter 2

Bless-ed

We raised four wonderfully active children, born close together so they could learn to share life with all its variables. In our county, there were two very large parks that were amazing in scope and variety, each a reflection of the other. It was as if a mechanical engineering team were given free rein to think like children and create as vastly as they could possibly imagine. Every type and kind of play equipment was brought into the mix, creating a plethora of wonder and delight for any and all who would partake. Large, long tubes to slide down and through to freedom. Bars of all shapes and sizes to climb and conquer. Zip lines and swings large and small so as to fly into the wind and meet it head-on. A very large, sand-bottomed pond just deep enough to splash, romp, and play in without much risk. Umbrellas, picnic tables, and fire pits to enjoy a meal in the afternoon sun. There was all of this and more to play away the day. It was delightful!

Years later, having moved on to a different location, I awoke to a dream one morning that included this park in all its grandeur. In the dream, the Lord showed me a little boy sitting on one of the diggers, scooping and moving sand from one pile to another and back again. He sat there for quite some time, not so much content as he was lacking the spark, the joy, the confidence, and the motivation needed to discover and explore the rest of the park. Perhaps he was simply unaware. But more likely he was simply afraid to venture out. Either way, as I watched this young boy, the Lord began to show me that this scene was the exact condition of the Church at large. He said, "My Kingdom is so vast, so amazing, so delightful. I have created so much for you. I have so much love for you, all of you who will receive. I have so much desire to share with you, and all of us together. And yet so many who know me do not partake." Stuck. So many are so stuck. It's a sad testimony, really.

In all my years walking with Jesus, with all the awe and wonder, with all the struggles, hardship, and difficulties, I have come fully to the understanding that this walk is intended to be an *adventure.* Allow me to unpack that statement. I came to know Jesus in my late twenties, with my wife and her sister by my side. I came from a sordid background with significant pain and woundedness; this is not the place to unpack that. The transformation from heathen to heaven was overwhelmingly amazing and remarkable. It was not heaven literally, but it certainly was quite heavenly. Jesus saved me from myself and from all the consequences of all my actions and reactions throughout the years. I quickly fell in love. I quickly fell into a love relationship that to this day has never ceased to amaze me, to repeatedly overwhelm me. I have come to know the wonder of who he is, the wonder of his love. As he has so patiently and graciously worked with me and all my inner turmoil, I have also come to clearly see the difficulties of this life, both those I have created and those that have been exercised against me. Within the whole of that came, and still remains, this wonder and understanding of the relational adventure he created and has invited all of us to join him in.

One of the joys of life in Colorado is whitewater rafting. Now there is an adventure, especially in early summer when the mountain snow is still melting and the very cold water is still high and rushing! I went over the side of the raft one time. Yikes! But more on that later. What is it about the activity of being seriously jostled around while banging, bumping, and bouncing down an aggressive, mostly out-of-control river that makes it an adventure, that makes it adventurous? Albeit calculated, it is the risk of it. It is the instability, the un-assuredness of it. It is the potential of endangerment. Seen another way, it is the fear of it. The uncertainty of what is happening in the moment, coupled with the uncertainty of what may come, produces a dimension of fear in the soul. It is not necessarily a bad thing; we (mostly) laugh our way downstream.

There is an interesting component of our humanity seen here. Those willing to step into the unknown will know. They will know the level of joy that comes from that fear, that comes only from taking that risk! Those unwilling will simply watch from the shore, from a distance, the joy others are having. The difference is a big deal. It is not that the watcher is wrong. It is that the engager is living, experiencing life at a deeper level. In this illustration, I would suggest the watcher is living the good that is not the best. The invitation, the encouragement from the Lord is to be the engager. The Lord wants to live the best with us. Perhaps the better way to say that is the Lord wants us to live the very best with him. He is quite the adventurer, and he is so inviting!

[Selah]

Life with him lived to the full, which he offers and promises (John 10:10b), comes with risk. One of my mentors said it this way: "How do you spell faith? R-i-s-k!" There is a huge challenge found here. The best comes not only at significant risk but also at great price—and at great sacrifice of self. It requires a willingness, a heart position, that gets to counting the cost and comes through the counting to that place wherein cost is no longer a consideration or a factor. Perhaps it is like going all in in a game of poker. Perhaps it is like jumping out of a plane with a parachute strapped to your back. Perhaps it is a full and total release of self's part in a personal relationship, making one very vulnerable. Perhaps it is sacrificing your insistence on your own want and need for that of another. Perhaps that other is the Lord Jesus. However it looks, it is very costly—and very rewarding.

Once, over a seven-month span, I was living in California while my family was in Colorado. I was able to make it home once a month for forty-eight hours. That was it, for seven months. It was a difficult time. On one of those occasions, there was a major blizzard in my home area; several counties were affected. The plane I was on was forced to land in a town some sixty miles away, and it was clear we were stuck there for as long as it would take for the blizzard to pass through and the road crews to clean it up; definitely it would be overnight and perhaps well into the following day. About two hours into this deviation from the plan, while standing around in the airport and minding my own business, someone came up from behind me and gave me a huge hug. Quite surprised because I didn't know anyone from the plane that well, I turned to see my wife! That smile, that sparkle in her eye when she looks at me, has been a melting point for me for now forty-three years! She drove through a blizzard to connect with me and bring me the rest of the way home. The entire area was shut down. A blizzard is high winds and heavy snow. There would have been very poor, perhaps no visibility while driving on roads deep with snow and unplowed. If she were to lose control and hit the ditch, she could have been there for hours, maybe a whole day. There have been times when people died in those conditions! Was she afraid? You know she was. Yet at the same time, she was not letting that risk, that fear, become a deterrent. Her thoughts, her focus, and her intents were not at all on her or her circumstances. They were on her man, and there is where the adventure came about! (We made it home safe and sound. Of course, I got elected to drive the second half of that trip!)

If my eyes are on the Lord and never on me, then let the games begin! If my perspective of any given situation are and remain in him; if my insights or assumptions, understandings or conclusions of any instance or circumstance are and remain in him, then fear is no longer an issue. Is there risk and fear? Sure. How could there not be? It is simply no longer a point of focus, no longer a constraint. The only way around fear is through it. Because perfect love drives out fear (1 John 4:18), and that would be the love of Jesus, the Perfect One, then when I am living fully in him and his presence, it becomes moot; fear and it companions have no place.

Risk, fear—these things can stand in the way of the richness he intends. Faith, trust—these things replace. Where we are going on this trip through the Beatitudes will bring us from the one to the other.

There is another thought from this trip down the whitewater rapids. To take away most of the uncertainty is to take away most of the risk. For the guides, the ones managing and controlling that raft, although the joy of the flight downriver remains, for the most part the adventure has dissipated. Why? They have hundreds and hundreds of trips down that river. They are familiar with it. There is a certain level of comfort that has been obtained, and so for them most of the risk is gone.

There is an element of risk in adventure that stirs excitement and joy—and the ongoing desire to experience it again. For all the years we have been married, the adventure has never gone out of our relationship. It's not because we create risk or fear but because we create adventure. We pursue, and thus we perpetrate this adventure in and for each other. Consequently, it never gets boring, routine, or ho-hum. And so it is with the Lord. It seems that for many, the element of the need for comfort, or the element of fear, has taken away the adventure of our walk with him and its joy and perhaps replaced it with a sense of boredom, or lethargy. The truth is we will forever be with him, and it will never get old, monotonous, or boring. The truth is he wants that adventure, that excitement for and with us, on this side of glory as well as on the other.

The Father created us for relationship, ultimately as the (spiritual) bride for his son, Jesus, the Bridegroom.[1] Think about that for a moment. Think about the realm of adventure there. The Adventurous One created us for adventure with him! The hint of the unknown, the risk, and the fear bring exhilaration, excitement, and immense joy. And when shared, there's great fulfillment. That is his heart. That is his purpose for and with us. That is his call to his people. We often get stuck in the pain, the hardship, the difficulty, which is very understandable. He is not stuck there. He is stuck on us and is continually inviting us into the adventure. The Beatitudes, fully engaged and applied, bring this adventure, this immense joy.

How he accomplishes this is truly a mystery beyond our understanding, because it seems so very backward. We live in a Kingdom—his. We are governed by the rules of a Kingdom—his. We are subject to the King. He is the King; we are not. His ways are not our ways. But they produce phenomenal results! The rest of this book intends to break this down into understandable, manageable truth. Bon appetit!

Bless-ed

"Bless-ed" is the first word in each of the Beatitudes, so here is yet another first in the stream of first things. There is the first point of communication, the Sermon on the Mount. It is the most important. Then there is the first part of the first point of communication, which are the Beatitudes. They are the most important of the most important. And here is the first word of the first part of the first point of communication: bless-ed. What a way to begin!

The definition of this word in this context is so very indicative of the Author. His heart is all about his creation, his kids! He is ever willing and wanting to give and give and give, to pour out from his heart of love and compassion. He is blessing, he is a blessing, and he loves to bless. Here, the word means favored, to be favored; it is honored, to be honored; it is esteemed highly, to be highly esteemed.

It is important to understand what our word is not. It does not mean "happy" or "blissful," as it has often been translated. It is way beyond a warm, fuzzy emotional expression. "Bless-ed is not happy, which is an emotion based on outward circumstances. Bless-ed here refers to the ultimate well-being and distinctive spiritual joy of those who share in the salvation of the Kingdom of God, [who share in deep relationship with the King]."[2]

To fully grasp the meaning and impact of this word, it must be seen that in this context, the word is a verb, which is to say it is a word of action, of engagement. It is not at all in a casual or informal state, and neither is it temporary. Rather, it is emphatically intentional and brings one to "a permanent state of being."[3] The Lord is not being nonchalant. True to his character, he is in full pursuit mode—and it is always you he is pursuing!

Even the grammar supports this pursuit. In this context, the word is what is called a predicate adjective. Say what? Okay, it may have been awhile since tenth grade English class! Basically, it is an adjective (adjectives are in the noun family) in a nominative state (a type of noun) that is given a predicative (a verb) form. This is done for emphasis. In that form, the word then makes an assertion. It is emphatic, highly accentuated.

Let me give you an example. I was one of the leaders of a men's group that met weekly for many years. Another one of the leaders, Kevin (who did not drink coffee), was often trying to empty the pot by continually offering more to those drinking. He was even a bit pushy about it. (He had no concept of ratios!) If you were the receptor of this push, you had more coffee in your cup. You could say that you had been coffee-ed. Because Kevin was the source of the action, you could also say you had been Kevin-ed and that the one behind the action was Kevin. The word "Kevin-ed" would be a predicate nominative, a noun given a verb form, put into a place of action. "Bless-ed" here is the same. It is an adjective offered as a verb. And it is made so by the one behind the adjective, behind the action: God. (Sidebar: As the word in our Beatitudes is in a predicate form, it comes into English not as "blessed" but as "bless-ed." The latter expresses it as the action word it is.)

All of this is to make clear the point as to whom it is doing the blessing. It is God; it is God's action and his alone. The action has nothing to do with the receptor. I got more coffee through no action or effort of my own. It is a demonstration from God of his character, herein expressing the quality of him, his heart, and his love toward his creation, toward you. Again, God is blessing, God is a blessing, and God loves to bless. In his love for you, he would have you be full and fully satisfied—not by the circumstances of life, and not by the fulfillment of the conditions found within the Beatitudes, but by the indwelling of the Christ, in whom these characteristics are found.

The predicate nature of the word stirs, draws, and appeals to those who meet this decisive revelation, this definitive invitation, in genuine hunger and with genuine faith (see Matthew 16:17; Luke 1:45). To those who accept this revelation and invitation without objection and with no false demands and no selfish maneuverings, they will know this fullness.

Thus, to be bless-ed is to be favored, honored, and highly esteemed by Jesus. It is an action from Jesus, found in the midst of a relationship with Jesus and resulting in being fully satisfied through Jesus.

[Selah]

Let's read that again. To be bless-ed is to be favored, honored, and highly esteemed by God, which is an action from God, found in the midst of a relationship with God and resulting in being fully satisfied through God. Wow!

Here, to be bless-ed is "the state of the believer in Christ, on account of Christ" (Matthew 5:11) for the sake of Christ, the Son of Man (Luke 6:22). It is to be "indwelt by Christ,"[4] the result of which is complete and absolute fullness and satisfaction within one's entire being. It is "the state of being marked by fullness from God."[5] It is "possessing the favor of God."[6] Favor speaks to graciousness and kindness. It means to bestow, which is to present as a gift, or simply to give. It is this: in graciousness to bestow graciousness, in kindness to bestow kindness. But there is more. To favor is to bestow to or upon an inferior. That would be us!

It makes me cry. The Creator of the Universe is here giving his gracious kindness, his heart if you will, to us, his created ones. In this we then possess the blessings; one could safely say we are possessed by the blessings. It is truly beyond words, beyond earthy description. It is a relationship so unfathomable, so amazingly splendid.

The one who is bless-ed is the privileged recipient of divine favor. This is so understated, so minimized, so belittled, and consequently so misunderstood in our culture, certainly in the Church culture. We often don't consider ourselves privileged. We do not consider and believe we are the actual recipients of God's favor. Yet it is so true. This word, and the reception of the truth it brings, indicates the state or condition of the believer in Christ who becomes a partaker of God's very nature. This comes by way of faith, through a walk of faith with him, found in the midst of his kingship, his Kingdom. "It is the equivalent to having God's Kingdom fully within one's heart, [one's life, wherein life's] satisfaction comes only [and solely] from God."[7] And it's not even remotely from circumstances or situations outside this relationship. Wow! I want to live there!

The bless-ed are near to God. They trust God. They hope and wait for God. They revere and love God. They are "the ones who are in the world yet independent of the world."[8] This is because they are in the Kingdom and live in full dependency upon the King. "Therein we live, and move, and have our being" (Acts 17:28). As these Beatitudes begin to unfold, one can start to see the power and significance within—and the invitation and need to capture that and live it out.

Chapter 3

The poor in spirit

The standard procedure in writing a chapter title is to capitalize the primary words in the title. I have purposely not done that here. As the chapter unfolds, you will recognize the reasoning behind this. Suffice it to say that the lowercase lettering clearly represents the message these words are expressing.

"Bless-ed are the poor in spirit, for theirs is the Kingdom of heaven" (Matthew 5:3).

I believe a life with Jesus is designed and intended to bring us to ever deeper places in him relationally. As I have stated earlier, I believe we have been created for just this. There are probably an infinite number of truths (John 14:6) coming from his heart, which he works into us over the course of a life with him, on this side and the other. To me, at this point in my life, there are three that stand out above the rest. There are three things he will work into my soul, my heart, and my spirit that he will have me living in and living out: patience, humility, and his glory. I also believe that the first two being worked simultaneously will reveal the third. It does not work in any other order. The truth found in this Beatitude takes us there.

The true and pure definition of the word *poor* here is not as you may suppose, not as it has so readily been offered and understood. "Poor dog, he is so mangy looking right now!" "Poor guy, he worked so hard and so wanted that victory!" "That is a poor excuse for a paint job on my car!" "Let's find a way to help them out; they are in a very poor spot right now." These are all good examples of the use of the word *poor*. None of them come close to what our word means and how it is being used in this context.

Here, the word is intense. It means "to be in a continuous state of destitute;"[1] it is "to cringe,"[2] "to cower, to cower down or hide."[3] It is "a poverty-stricken condition, a state of severe lack."[4] It would be "to bow down timidly."[5] This timidity is coming from an overwhelming sense of inability and a subsequent sense of insignificance. Here, poor in spirit refers to those who recognize their spiritual helplessness; it is the first step to blessedness.[6]

In 1 Kings there is the story of Elijah and the widowed woman (1 Kings 17:7f). The bottom line of the story is this: She has very little. She has lost her husband, her primary means of support. During an extreme famine in the land, she is down to her last cup of flour and last ounce of oil. In her heart, it is her intention to cook one more meal and then die. The meaning of poor in our text would be the condition of this woman after she had eaten that meal. In that state, she has nothing, and she has no natural ability to obtain anything. That is our word.

Poor here means helpless. It does not mean having nothing, but with the ability to work, borrow, or even steal something. No, this definition, this circumstance, is such that there is no way, no ability, no scheme of attaining anything—ever. The full essence of the meaning of the word does in fact come into English not as poor but as "fully helpless." It's truly, entirely, and completely without any opportunity or ability to get or gain or have. There are five Hebrew and three Greek words that translate into English as *poor.* Only one—this one, used sparingly in Scripture—speaks to this. It is not weak but with ability. It is not a temporary condition that I can work my way out of, figure out, or manage my way through. No, it is helpless. Period.

This is where the Lord would have us be, to live with and in him all the days of our lives.

[Selah]

To engage this, to allow the Lord to work this into our lives, brings us to nothingness. His hand, his work here puts us into a state of total dependency. That is the point. It is the baby duckling that would drown or starve to death without the aid of its mother. It is any baby or young child or special-needs adult without the constant assistance of someone who can provide food and shelter, protection and love. It's absolute and unmitigated dependency. It is me in the whitewater rafting predicament I mentioned in the previous chapter, except not temporarily but forever: I was one of the front men in a raft with ten people in it going down a series of level four and level five rapids on the Arkansas River one wonderfully warm, early summer day. (Remember in chapter 2 when I was "being seriously jostled around while banging, bumping, and bouncing down an aggressive, mostly out-of-control river!") My feet were securely planted because they were the pivot point for the intense paddling we were doing to keep ourselves in a mostly upright and downriver position—and to keep from going face first into the rocks that were straight ahead! I'm not sure if we hit a rock just under the surface of the water or just a serious wave, but out of nowhere my foot slipped, and I was in the water! It took more time to write that sentence than it did for me to be in and under the water. (Is this still an adventure, or have we crossed over to sheer panic?) I was helpless. There was absolutely nothing, not one thing, I could do to save myself. Whatever was going to happen next was fully outside my ability to accomplish. I was truly helpless. That is our word, only not just for the moment or a season but forever. This word, and the principle behind it, is still another first in our journey.

The first Old Testament book written was Job. The reason it was first is because of the critical importance of the overriding message within its contents. It is first by intention, which makes all that follows subject to it. That means all of God's Kingdom life comes from this essential foundational piece. What the text and the Lord has shown me is this: Job was a righteous man who loved God. God wanted, and so intended, to go deeper and have with Job the deepest Creator-created relationship possible. There were things within Job's heart preventing that from becoming a full reality. Like the rest of us humans, Job had issues. Consider spiritual pride. God, in his infinite love for his own and in his infinite wisdom, pointed out Job to Lucifer (Job 1:8). Why would our loving God do such a thing? Simply put, to get to the bottom of Job's heart in order to heal it. He sought to expose the issues at hand and remove them so as to heal him. That is where the connection is the deepest, strongest, and most powerful. That is the only way to get us to the place we were all created for in the first place: the place of bottomless, immeasurably rich relationship with Jesus, the Lord and Savior.

In order to completely comprehend and embrace the manner of God's dealings, one must grasp and understand several things about God. "His ways are not our ways, [but are far superior for a far superior purpose]" (Job, chapters 38, 39). The devil is a tool and nothing more, used by God to "buffet" us, which is a good King James phrase and means "to contend or battle against" (Isaiah 54:16–17). The Lord disciplines those he loves (Hebrews 12:6, 10b). The reason for the discipline is to make us disciplined; it is the same root word. The reason to be disciplined is to make us disciples—still the same word. The reason for being made disciples is to bring us to places of indescribable commitment and dedication in our love relationship with him. He will take us to the place of brokenness and a contrite heart and life in order to bring us to the richness and completeness found therein (Psalm 51:17; Isaiah 57:15b).

Said another way, the reason for all of that is this: It is the only way we come to the deep places, the deepest of deep places, in and with him, which is always his desire for and with us. We are to deny ourselves, take up our cross and carry it, and follow him (Matthew 10:38, 16:25). To take up one's cross and follow is to yield oneself in total commitment to Jesus. To carry that cross is to remain in that yielded, committed, dedicated position. To deny oneself is to deny one's self. It is to forego the things that comprise the inner man with all its wants and demands, with all its baggage. This is your self, the self within you, the self that comprises you, that must be denied and put to death (Romans 8:13; Colossians 3:5). This is your way, your will, your want, your aspirations and agenda, your plans and goals.

This is a very difficult message. We do not want to change, not if we are being honest about ourselves and our lives. Change is difficult, no doubt. And denying the inner man to that place of death of self, of death to self, is difficult. It is not pretty. We all die ugly. But die we must, if we will live to the fullness of the Lord's desire and intent for us. "For whoever wants to save his life will lose it, but whoever loses his life for my sake will find it" (Matthew 16:25). Perhaps this verse is more clearly understood from the Amplified Bible: "For whoever is bent on saving his [temporal] life [his comfort and security here] shall lose it [eternal life]; and whoever loses his life [his comfort and security here] for my sake shall find it [life everlasting] [and life to its fullness here]" (Matthew 16:25).

The truth is I cannot help myself. I cannot fix myself. I cannot get myself out of the duplicitous quandary, the guile, the miry clay, the quicksand I find myself in, try as I may. And I have tried repeatedly, ad nauseam. You too, I expect. It matters not how I got there, not really; it only matters how I get out. I can read all the Christian self-help books on the planet. That will work. "For a minute!"[7] I can change my behavior, but that won't hold for long. That is because the need for behavior modification is not found in my behavior. It is found in and comes from my heart. And my heart, like yours, is "desperately wicked and deceitful above all things" (Jeremiah 17:9). Thus the need for a change agent, for the Change Agent, the Savior, the Lord. It is imperative here to pause a moment and catch up to this: There is a grace found here provided by the One who gives grace freely. As has been mentioned, all that he requires of us, he provides for us within. The call, the command, is truly the toughest, most challenging directive we will ever hear from the Lord. His grace is sufficient, is all sufficient in its abundance. He does not ever leave us alone in this, or any, endeavor.

The overriding message in Job is simple: I am God and you are not (Job 38–39). I hear the Lord saying, "I love your dearly; so much I was willing to sacrifice my Son for you; so much I am willing to take the time and the effort to work my heart into yours.

I created you out of this love and for a deep, ever deeper, love relationship. My ways are good and wonderful and without need for change (1 Samuel 15:29; Hebrews 7:21). I want you deep with me; I want you in the depths of my heart. I must do my work in you for that to happen. I know what I am doing, I am faithful, and I will accomplish and finish all I set out to do in you, for you, and for us together (Philippians 1:6)."

The book of Job is the first for good reason, for God's good reason. It sets the table for all that follows. It is saying, "I am God. If you ask me in, I am your God. You are helpless. I have taken and will take care of you. I am your protection (shield, strong tower), your provider, your strength. I go before you and behind you. I am all around you. I love you and long for you. We will spend eternity together! You must learn to yield to me, to my ways. You must learn that I am your Lord and King, which makes you my servant. There is wonderful joy in this, as we walk through forever together."

[Selah]

As Job is the first written Old Testament book and brings clearly this message, so is James the first written New Testament book, and it brings the same message. James was the half-brother of Jesus, the eldest of those fathered by Joseph. Early on, he was one of those who said Jesus was out of his mind (Mark 3:21). He was also part of the family who did not believe in him, who doubted (John 7:5). Yet after the crucifixion, resurrection, and ascension of Jesus, James become very much like his brother, now his Christ. Over time he became the chief elder statesman of the church in Jerusalem and the leader of the Jerusalem council (Acts 15:13, 21:18). Toward the end of his life, in the seasoned wisdom and revelation that only comes from a life of allowing the Lord to be his Lord, he was used to pen the book of James. (Some have said, as he so emulated Jesus in the whole of his life, and as this book so closely brings his message to the table, that the letter should have been labeled "The Gospel of Jesus.")

His letter speaks straight up from this wisdom, this revelation. "Consider it pure joy, my brothers, whenever you face trials of many kinds, because you know that the testing of your faith develops perseverance. Perseverance must finish its work so that you may be mature and complete, not lacking anything" (James 1:2–4).

The operative words in this passage are *trial* and *testing*. Trial means "a putting to proof," whereas testing is "the means of [that] proving." Trial comes from two words, "to test" and "to pierce."[8] It is found in the same family of words that speak to learning. It is "to learn the nature or character of someone by submitting [to that same someone,] to thorough and extensive testing."[9] There are two important words in this definition: *character* and *thorough*. There is the intention of resolve, of resolution and completion, within this word. This is the Lord allowing us to be tried and tested for the sole purpose of building us up to that place of maturity and completeness. He is quite extensive and completely thorough in bringing us to this position in him of lacking nothing. The reason behind this work must be seen and understood so as to be fully embraced. Just as it was in Job, it is the love God has for his creation, the desire he has for intimacy with his own, that drives him. The degree to which he can bring us to maturity and completeness is directly proportionate to the degree in which we are in depth of intimacy with him; ever more complete, ever deeper.

Perhaps the way the word is used in the Septuagint says it best. The word primarily implies "a testing of a partner in a covenant relationship to see whether they are keeping their side of the agreement."[10] This is not to catch us doing something wrong. This is not to trip us up and then find fault. To the contrary, this is to bring us so very close. It is Father doing the exact same thing that was taking place with Job: bringing out what needed to come out so as to bring in what he wanted within. In some ways, perhaps, it looks like a stress test found in the midst of a diagnostic procedure, stressing a component to find its weakness. Although in this case, it is not the diagnostician applying stress to determine what will break and thus need repair. Rather, it is Father already fully aware of the areas of weakness, applying pressure for the purposes of restoration, for the purposes of thorough and complete character development. It is redemptive. When we yield to all of this, and when we engage the Lord in the heat of all this and allow him his work, we come to the place of complete maturity and fullness of joy.

Both these books align fully and directly with the heart of the Beatitudes, starting with the hard reality that we are helpless. It is a hard reality. It is also an amazingly freeing reality. It is here that we discover that blessedness, that favor, that divine favor found nowhere else. It is here that pride and rebellion, with all of their disgusting manifestations, leave. I can only be free in this life when I am no longer in charge. As soon as I decide to take control, I also take burden. And when I do that, it instantly becomes fear and pride and rebellion—and all their entrails, all the elements of the flesh, human nature, and sin nature that bog me down. Baggage. When I bow to Jesus in head, heart, and action, I release myself to him, I become fully his. Then I am fully free in him. In all honesty, this is the only way to the fullness of life he has offered and promised. No other way works, not really. I think that to think otherwise is just fooling oneself. In all reality, we are helpless without him anyway—we just think we're not! Perhaps it is best to yield to being helpless in him, with him, instead of continuing to try to build and live our lives our own way.

Jesus lived here. Remember, the Beatitudes are all character traits of the Christ. He learned to live here. He came to Earth as a man, having set aside his deity (Philippians 2:7; Hebrews 2:17). He became helpless for our sake. Second Corinthians 8:9 says, "For you know the grace of our Lord Jesus Christ, that though he was rich, yet for your [our] sakes he became poor [helpless], so that you through his poverty might become rich." This passage has nothing to do with money or anything in the natural realm and everything to do with the heart and the spiritual realm. He learned obedience—that is, full obedience—to his Father through the suffering he endured (Hebrews 5:8). Yes, that suffering is seen in his love and care for us humans, and certainly on the Cross. But it is also seen within all of the struggles he encountered day by day. He endured much hardship by way of conflict, both internal and external, with those who came against him. He dealt with tremendous rejection from family, from friends, from enemies. He knew tremendous loneliness. He had great turmoil within. He was labeled the man of sorrows (Isaiah 53:3). And yet he did not rise up in pride, in self-defense, or in any form of self-protection or preservation. Instead, recognizing what Father was wanting and intending to accomplish in his heart, and recognizing and acknowledging his helplessness, he yielded and submitted to Father; hence came freedom, rest, joy, and peace. (This will be expounded on in chapter 5.)

From Job and James, and from this Beatitude, we see that the first move of God, the first concrete block in the foundation of life under his Lordship, is to remove self from the equation. By bringing self to nothing, he can bring us into the sweet place of total dependency, wherein we can be at our closest and deepest place with him. Jesus said it best in John 5:19 and again in 5:30 that "the Son can do nothing by himself; he can do only what he sees his Father doing, because whatever the Father does the Son also does." And then, "By myself I can do nothing." He is stating the choice he has made. He is relinquishing any and all control he may have, or thinks he may have, to the Father, to his Father. He is not his own. A bit later, he hung on the Cross for us. If we come to a life in him, if we say yes to him, we are saying yes to the truth that by his action on the Cross he redeemed us, he has purchased us. We belong to him. I am no longer my own; I belong to another and his name is Jesus. This whole life is about that. This whole eternity is about that. And it starts in earnest, in its intended fullness, when we come to the stark, true reality that we are helpless; our all is in his hands. And in that place we are bless-ed, favored, by God.

We want our way. We want to have control, to be comfortable, to flow through life in our way—and to ask God to bless it. But in the life he wants for us—which is the best life, the one defined by him, the one he intended when we were created, and that he intends for us now—he is Lord. He is the leader; we are the followers. It is all intended to be lived his way, never yours or mine. If that is the case, it must be the first thing, it must start right here, by realizing that we are truly helpless in the overall reality of things, of this life. He will work patience, humility, and his glory into our hearts. It starts here.

Remember, as was said earlier, "We are subject to the King. He is the King, we are not. His ways are not our ways. But they produce phenomenal results!"

Chapter 4

Those Who Mourn

Matthew 5:4 says, "Bless-ed are those who mourn, for they will be comforted."

To mourn... This is a very sensitive subject matter, at least in my heart. In my life, I have experienced much by way of struggle and difficulty, hurt and pain, brokenness and woundedness. There has been much mourning and sorrow. I often experience a sometimes overwhelming sense of sorrow. Perhaps you do too. Sometimes it feels like too much. Without any bias, prejudice, or judgment, I think it is safe to say that most every family or extended family has elements of these agonies. Certainly, that is true within my ministry and personal experiences. That makes me mournful. We would all like it to be different. We would all like life to be warm and fuzzy, safe and secure, comfortable and in control. Yet there are so many situations that we face that seem either partially or totally void of what is right and just, or at least what we think should be right and just. There are so many times where things don't seem to add up.

David knew of this. He lived it from boyhood and throughout his life. His life story is an excellent read and study; I highly recommend it.

To mourn in this context is to lament, to grieve, to be sorrowful or filled with sorrow.[1] It is to "experience sadness or grief as the result of depressing circumstances."[2] It is to grieve "with a grief which so takes possession of the whole being it cannot be hidden,"[3] and thus it is an overwhelming thing. It is internal, in the heart. There is an external expression found here as well, "a sorrow outwardly expressed in some way such as tears or laments,"[4] or "to travail."[5] These words speak to a deep sorrow. A synonym is "to beat the breast as an outward sign of an inner grief."[6] And to intensify things all the more, our word is a verb found in the present tense, which means it is a word of continuous action, an ongoing mourning.

Jesus knew of this. He lived it from boyhood and throughout his life. His life story is an excellent read and study; I highly recommend it!

Although mourning can be very much related to things personal, here it has more to do with things corporate, outside of self. It is sorrow that leads to repentance and brings us to Jesus in the first place (2 Corinthians 7:10). But mourning in this context is not remorse or repentance for my sin, my sin nature; it is broader than that. Remember that each Beatitude stands alone, but they also build on each other. Having come to the understanding and the place of helplessness, of living in that place of dependency on the Lord, the focus is no longer on my issues, my self; it is solely on the Lord and what is important to him. It is about Jesus, and about others. It is about his heart, his agenda. Here, to mourn is to be in mourning for someone or something apart from self. It has more to do with the bigger picture, the broader perspective, perhaps "the overall condition of humanity."[7]

It needs to be recalled, in light of the overshadowing point of focus within all the Beatitudes, just where the emphasis lies. As was stated earlier, Jesus said in Matthew 5:11 a phrase: "on account of me. [For my sake.]" So Jesus is the focus here. This mourning, then, is not me mourning over my life and circumstances, although it does include me. This has to do with him, with the mourning coming from his heart. It is mourning with and for the sake of Christ. Isaiah 53:3 says that Jesus was a man of sorrow. The text says fully, "He was a man of sorrows, and familiar with suffering." Our word, in its context, is mourning with him over the things that cause him sorrow. We are highly favored when we couple with him in that.

Herein lies an aspect of walking with Jesus that is not very familiar to most believers. It is not considered and communicated very often, yet it is a large component within his heart. So just what is this "Bless-ed are those who mourn"? What is with that? What is the value, the purpose of mourning, of grief and sorrow in this context? It is actually designed to be a motivator, a heart motivator.

Remember that this is all about relationship in a vertical stance between us and the Lord, and then in a horizontal posture between us and others. Relationship assumes communication, which is only activated when an exchange or dialogue happens between at least two different beings. This brings interaction, which produces the sharing of life, of community. Also, to be empty of self opens the heart to see, and so take on, the struggle of others. This is one of the components within the relational experience to which we are called. Coming to the tangible place of dependency frees self from the picture, from the scene. This not only opens the soul but sensitizes it to all that is around: the presence of the Lord and the challenge of those in view. With this comes not self's burden but the Lord's. The essence of mourning has all to do with coupling with Jesus in burden, but also with his compassion to press in regarding these burdens. Jesus modeled much for us in the life he led while on this planet, and nothing less than his dependency on Father. Within this yieldedness came also the full and complete intimacy with the Father, which then brings the rich compassion he found in the Father's heart. This compassion drove Jesus (Matthew 14:14), and it is meant to accomplish the same in us. It is intended that Father, Jesus, Holy Spirit, and all of us flow together in the same vein of love and compassion, one for the other and all for the many in need. Of course, we have not yet come above the need ourselves! But therein lies a wonderful truth: Even though we have not yet arrived, and thus still have need, we can join with the Lord in helping, in being used by him to bring help to others in their time of need. That help starts with mourning over that need.

An important part of this life, according to what is readily seen in Scripture, is the lament. Throughout history and in most every culture is found some expression of this. In Hebraic culture, from Genesis and on, is found the "sapad," the "qadar," the "qina,"[8] and other terms, all giving definition to the expressions of grief and sorrow, crying, weeping, and groaning over the struggles and hardships of life, both personal and corporate. At one point there were even professional mourners! They were hired to contribute more demonstration and emphasis to the grieving process in a death, loss, or serious illness within a family unit. Some laments were even national in scale, such as with King David. The Psalms are full of laments. Job and Micah, Isaiah and Jeremiah, and many others were well-known for their laments. A lament is not a gripe session or a grumble-and-complain meeting. It is an honest and sincere cry of the heart over something of significance that is hard and difficult within life. Jesus mourned; he lamented. In John 11:35 it says, "Jesus wept." What was he weeping about or over? This question prompts yet another: What is it that Jesus came to Earth for in the first place? Didn't he come to die for us so that we wouldn't have to, so that we could have life now and forever (John 3:16, 36 KJV)? The immediate context of the John 11:35 passage is the death of Lazarus, whom Jesus was about to raise from the dead, and the subsequent sorrow within his family. But this story is much bigger than that. It is prophetic of all of humanity. Lazarus is symbolic of the death that threatens all of us, all of creation. The greater context is Jesus weeping over the condition, the physical and spiritual death of us all that will come or would come without his intervention and ensuing salvation.

Now enters the element of intercession. As we follow and progress through the Beatitudes, we take steps. Having been brought to that place of understanding our need and our dependency, now the building, the progression begins. And where better than intercession? To intercede is to intervene for the purpose of producing agreement. It is "to intervene in order to plead or argue on behalf of another."[9] It is "to impinge or to confer with so as to affect."[10] Jesus is the Chief Intercessor. He is constantly in an attitude and position of intercession before the Father on behalf of all of his created ones (Hebrews 7:25). This is who he is. This is what he does. He laments. He cries out. He presses in to the Father on our behalf, for all of us—whether or not we walk with him. We are in trouble. We need help. There is evil and ugly all around. He cries out "because of wickedness and oppression."[11] The things that make him weep and mourn are the things he intercedes over and about. To be in an attitude, a frame of reference, of mourning is to be as Jesus is. It is his love, his compassion that drives him to travail over his future bride—his fiancée, if you will. Again, this is who he is, and within the context of this Beatitude, this is what he is inviting us to. Mourning is seeing and realizing the plight of us humans and then grieving and lamenting over that. When the motivating factor of compassion is added, it creates intercession. We are here invited to join him in mourning and in interceding over the state of ourselves, our fellow brothers and sisters, and all the people around the world for whom he prompts us to intercede. Yes, Jesus wept. One of the definitions of our word mourn is "to weep."[12] From that he was consumed and thus driven by compassion for us (Matthew 9:36). It is today as it was then. As is the invitation.

[Selah]

Another question arises when we consider mourning and its place in the Beatitudes, one I believe is common to all. What is it that draws, or sometimes even drives, us to withdraw? Why is it that we disengage or disconnect, discount ourselves, even dismiss ourselves from life, from Jesus? What is it that can actually drive us to darkness? It is not the devil; he can simply exercise what already exists within us (John 14:30). Certainly, he can work to try to embellish and amplify what is, but he does not create it, he is not the source of it. So just what is it, then? The brokenness of our souls is seemingly ever present in our world, both today and throughout history. It may be more apparent at some times than it is at others, but it is ever present. It is the root reason why we need a savior, our Savior. It is called sin. It is called the sin nature. It is often referred to as iniquity.

I believe there is a disconnect in our soul from two sources. One is this thing called sin. Sin separates us from God. Interestingly enough, it does not separate him from us, but its result does place a wedge, a division, between us and him. Confession and repentance can and do restore us to him, especially if we are faithful to do so as often as we need. The other is that we have been created in such a way that there is a void, an empty space, which is then an emptiness, in our soul that by design can be filled only by him. The natural man, the one without the knowledge of God in his heart (Proverbs 2:5; Ephesians 4:13; see note one at chapter's end), reads this void through the lens of fear and consequently enters into sin, into some sinful activity, to pacify his angst. By default, that discounts him. The result is a disconnected soul, which breeds more sin. Said another way, the net result of being sinned against is to sin.

When I came to Jesus, all of my sin issues—my baggage, if you will—came with me. He offered me a life with him, a life without end in his presence. He offered me a life full of his love, his gentle Spirit, and his glory. He died for my sin, yes (Romans 6:1–11). That puts me in the position of being perfect while being made perfect (Hebrews 10:14). Yet he did not immediately remove all of my baggage. No, he removed much and left the rest for he and I to work through together. This is the tangible reality of sanctification.[13] When Yahweh gave the promised land to the Israelites, he said clearly that he was not giving the entire land to them all at once. "[It is yours], but not all at once, lest the wild animals multiply against you" (Exodus 23:29, Amplified). In other words, it is theirs as he unfolds it at his pace and discretion. He offered it in this manner to protect them from others and even from themselves. So it is with us and our walk with Jesus. Again, this process is called sanctification, and it is designed to be lifelong.

I still have some baggage. I have been healed and set free of much, but I am still in process; I still have a way to go. You too, I expect. Thus, there remains these elements of baggage, of iniquity, of sin past and even present. And from that comes this propensity to disconnect myself from my Lord from time to time. The upside is that he uses this mess to bring me closer to him as he heals me from it. That is his intention for all of us. The downside is we don't always see or understand what he is doing, and so we get discouraged. There lies the disconnect. Enter the King, in all his compassion and care. He turns things about, uses our mess to heal us, and draws us close to him in thankfulness and adoration. Only God can change something so ugly into something so beautiful on our behalf. It is for his glory and our gain. He does not create the mess; we live in a fallen world and can produce our own without any help. The sin and the sin nature of mankind has been present and active from day one, and it certainly abounds today. No, he does not create all of the baggage in our hearts, but he does use it, and in that he does change us (Romans 8:28).

What does this have to do with mourning? This disconnect, this separation creates a tension, an ache even, in our souls, in our minds and spirits, and even in our bodies. There is a gap between where we live and where the Lord would have us to live (where he desires we live with him), and we know it (Romans 1:19–20). We know of the gap, and we know of his desire for us. We perhaps don't know it well or understand it fully, but that knowing is resident in the heart. It is precisely that knowing that generates the tension—again, that ache. And that causes us to mourn. When we are made aware of not just our dilemma but that of those around us, we are then drawn to mourn for them too.

Bless-ed are those who mourn. Bless-ed are those who so align with the heart of Jesus that they become one with him in the dependency upon Father and the intimacy of care, concern, and compassion for all those around, for his creation.

The following is from my journal, with a few interjections.

> I ache inside.
>
> There is a place the Lord would have us occupy. A place where he would have us live. It is within the understanding of abide (John 15), but more. It is to dwell, to reside with and in him. But it is also to wholly rest, to completely trust, to simply be in him. Here we are one. Here we are at a place beyond words. It is difficult to express. He wants me in him and him in me, but that is not it, not all of it. He wants me to be aware of him always. Not often. Not occasionally. Always. All the time. It is this: Jesus asked me to be his friend. He is mine; I get that. This is different. This is him asking me to be his friend with no agenda, with no plan or scheme; without it being need based. Just presence, just being. It is being enclosed *in* him but also *with* him. As I was meditating upon this invitation, Jesus drew me to Song of Songs 4:12, which speaks to "a garden enclosed." He said, "I close you in. I want you closed in. To me. In me. With me." Enclosed means "to close in on all sides."[14]
>
> Being enclosed here creates, and so brings about, two things. First, it brings safety and security, supplied by the Lord. Second, it brings strength and confidence produced by him and me together. The first deals with the fear, the weakness, and the insecurity found within me, which brings place to the second. The second is where Jesus is inviting, is wanting me to live. The first having been established, built, and maintained becomes not the

focus. The foundation now built, he and I move up and in to the deeper things of life with each other. It is the sweetest place in existence. It is well beyond the natural way, the natural means of life. It is friend and friendship beyond measure. (Proverbs 18:24). As per him. Defined not by me. Intimacy is good but incomplete in definition. Grand. Grandeur. Superlatives are too short, too shy of the mark. Exquisite. Extraordinarily exquisite. Knowing his thoughts, his heart. Knowing that he is knowing mine. [The word *know* needs to be expounded upon. Again, see note one.] Anticipating. Anticipatory. Presence. Heartbeat. Breath. Hearing his breath. Feeling the warmth of his breath, of his presence. Anticipating his being. Waking to him. Turning the corner to him. Bumping into him. Meeting with him on a walk at sunrise. Fun. Playful. Splash of cold water in the face on a hot day.[15] Joy. Deep calling unto deep. This place is beyond description, really. Sometimes, it seems that to try to articulate this depth actually diminishes it …

The rub: it comes at very high cost. Exquisite. Horrific. Wonderful. Heinous. It requires all, ongoingly all. It is all in. It is a denying of self, but more. It is denying to the extent of a death to self, true and complete, daily and in the moment. It is a life amazingly deep and rich. It comes no other way. Beautiful. Horrible. Jesus asked me to be his friend. I didn't even know what that meant, not in the depth of it. I knew he was my friend. But this is being his. He is mine. If I am obeying, if I am walking in his righteousness, I am his friend (John 14:23; James 2:23). Yes. But more. If it is even possible, much more. In general, he cannot trust mankind. He knows too much (John 2:24–25). He wants me to be a friend he can trust. Oh, my. With no agenda. With no motives, ulterior or not. With no pretense. Just friend. Just being. Loving, accepting, embracing, as is. This is the call. This is his heart. For me. For you. If I, if we will. High cost. Even higher value.

These beatitudes spell out that cost. Bless-ed are the helpless, are those who ache, are those who cry out, are those who are willing—and thus have been stripped of all self, all fear, all pride, all rebellion, and on. All. Today and tomorrow, and forever. And I still have not defined it. Trust beyond trust. Fear is evidenced in the garden, in Genesis, with Adam and Eve. It seems that pride and rebellion come from it. It is the root of our troubles within our humanity. Fear. Perfect love casts out fear (1 John 4:18). No fear. But not by way of some shallow commercial statement. No fear. All love, his. So overwhelmed, so blown away by that love there is no breath without it. There is no heartbeat without it. There is no step, no action, no essence without it. No fear. Just Jesus. Just Father. Just Holy Spirit. Just being. Breathing in him. Seeing. Tasting. Hearing. Touching. Smelling. Feeling. Being. In him. It is the vision of the bride-to-be dancing before her lover [See note two at chapter's end for an explanation of this vision.], which is so powerful, so beautiful beyond description. Free in him, free for him. Pure, so very pure. Holy in him. Righteous in him. Pure in her being, in her choice. We are that vision to him. He is bringing us there.

> I am spent. Exhausted, done in. On him. Spent on him. He is poured out over me, and me over him. All in, until there is nothing. All becomes nothing when spent on him. So intimate. A whisper, soft. A touch, gentle and tender.

Can we live here? "Is this a test?" "Yes." "If I pass, can I stay?" "Do you want to stay?" "Yes" "That's nice." (From *Bourne Legacy*, 2017). Only the Lord's answer is not "That's nice." It is an emphatic, excited "All right!" as he agrees with our yes. Can we live here? In the depth, in the peace that is well beyond understanding (Philippians 4:7), in the closeness that is closer than close? So close we need not ask? Yes, we can. Because we know. In the depth of the heart, if we are listening, if we are paying attention, we know. As he knows us before we are, before we talk or even breath, before we ask, so we know him. Before I even think to ask the question, I know the answer is a quiet, sweet, tender, gentle, deep, touching, resounding, absolute, emphatic yes. His presence, his love manifested brings overwhelmingly deep, deep joy.

[Selah]

Note One: Knowledge

There are several Greek words that translate into English as "know" or "knowledge," and of primary use there are two. They are *gnosis* and *epignosis*. Some would pronounce these words with the g active, while others would speak it with a silent *g*. Either way, the first one is rendered as knowledge, as in information, data, and facts; it is fragmentary, partial. It can also be intelligence or a natural form of understanding or wisdom. It might be understood as head knowledge, or a head knowledge. The second one is a more clear and exact knowledge. It is an applied knowledge; there is a thorough and complete participation in the knowledge. This form of the word is experiential; there is an engagement with the source of this knowledge. In our context, that source is most often the Lord God. There is an effect, an exerted influence found here. It often carries a relational dynamic with it. The difference between the two words is stark and needs to be captured.

There are many instances within both Old and New Testament where the difference between these words is clearly seen. One example is found in Genesis 4, where Adam *knew* Eve and a child was born. Adam did not just have some information about Eve, or she some facts about him. Although they did have an understanding about and with each other, they also had an applied knowledge that was participatory and experiential; they had a relational knowledge of and with one another. The word used specifically in the context of this journal entry, and generally in the context of this book, is definitely and definitively the latter word, *epignosis*.

Note Two: A Vision

In the context of some intense and extended time of worship and intercession, I had this vision. I saw the vision twice, several months apart.

I saw a young woman, tall and slender with long, flowing wavy hair. (First Corinthians 11:15 says that a woman's glory is her hair. From that, it could be said she was in her glory, but really, she was in His.) She was wearing a fluid gown that dropped gracefully to her ankles, fitted to the waist; the skirt was full and flowing. It was a rich and radiant white, with many sheer layers comprising its fullness. The qualities of her persona were majestic and strikingly beautiful in this delightfully stunning gown. She was dancing barefoot, stepping and twirling with an amazing freedom and joy. The sense of her movements was one of full abandon, with absolutely no hindrance or restriction. She was not abandoned from but freely abandoned into her dance—and the One for whom she was dancing. There was a remarkable, even incredible sense of purity about her. Although this vision initially could have been seen as something sensual, on the contrary, it became immediately apparent that this young woman was flowing entirely in a righteous and pure manner. Her attention was not at all on herself, and neither was she attempting to draw attention to herself. Head, heart, and action, she was immersed completely upon that One. Her dance, in all its splendor, was an intense, unadulterated engagement of intimacy, of worship with and to her Lover, her Lord.

Then the Lord revealed to me what I was seeing. It was a vision of the bride-to-be, the fiancée of the Bridegroom, in all her magnificence and glory, dancing with immense joy and excitement before her King. She was overwhelmingly in love with the one and only of her heart, and her actions captured in totality the delight within her heart.

This vision expresses a basic core value, the essence of God's heart: rich, deep, pure, intimate relationship; Jesus with his bride, in love beyond description, heart to heart forever. She is a picture of all who comprise his Kingdom. The bride of Christ (Isaiah 62:5; Revelation 19:7, 21:9, 22:17) is all of us who are born-again, who have said yes to Jesus and have stepped into the Kingdom. It is those who are seeking the Lord and King as he has instructed and directed. This vision is but a snapshot, a brief video at best, of what is in store for us with Jesus once we marry. The fullness of this vision is for the other side, for eternity; it is a spiritual reality. But it is also, albeit in a more limited manner, a spiritual actuality for this side, for this life.

Chapter 5

Prautes, Part One

Matthew 5:5 says, "Bless-ed are the meek, for they will inherit the earth."

It was in 1992 that I was first introduced to this word by Holy Spirit. I had been reading the Beatitudes periodically for over thirteen years as a believer by then. I had what I thought was a reasonably good understanding. But when the light came on, I began to understand what I did not understand. I have been studying it ever since. This one word has probably more highly impacted and affected my life and my walk with Jesus than any other single word in all of Scripture. Almost all of my revelation and comprehension of the Father and Jesus and their Kingdom comes through the heart of this word. Quite honestly, other than the fullness of the word *love,* I find this word, in its Greek and Hebrew origins, is more emphatically accurate regarding the definition and expression of the heart of Jesus than any other single word in the Word. That is a strong statement! He defines this word. He emulates this word. He is this word.

The word is so unique in its definition and subsequent meaning and understanding that it truly is not translatable into English. Said briefly—and I will expound on this as the chapter unfolds—the many words that have been and are used to translate *prautes* into English are not actually the word but the partial result of what the action of the word produces in the heart. Again, the word itself is not directly translatable.

The word in Greek is *prautes.* That is the noun; the adjective is *praus.* It is enunciated "prow-tees." The *o* in the first syllable is like the *o* in *ouch.* The *e* in the second syllable can be pronounced with a short or long *e.* More commonly, it is pronounced with the latter, and so the last syllable is "-tees" and rhymes with *peace*: prow-teace. Prautes it is.

To bring full definition and understanding to this word, it does us well to bring clarity to what it is not. There have been many translations, transliterations, paraphrases, and interpolations of the Word of God down through the centuries, more so in recent years. Many of these works are wonderful, but many are not; the latter potentially bring great confusion and subsequent difficulty to life. Recently, I told my wife that I am going to name our next dog Theology. That way when he does something wrong, I can say, "Bad Theology!" because there is so much of it out there! Much of it comes by way of "bad" interpretation. There are many inherent difficulties in this type of work because translating any one word from one language to another can be quite complicated. Within any language, any society, words tend to morph over time, and from that their meanings can change. (It has never ceased to amaze me, and it is yet another testimony to the faithfulness of

God, that through all the centuries of transcribing and translating the Scriptures, while any other writing would have morphed, the Word of God has not.) So to stay true to the original languages is remarkable work and very challenging. In addition, because our word does not translate directly into our language, the net result can be quite unclear and confusing.

Prautes does not mean humble; it does not mean power under control. It does not mean meek or mild, as those words now suggest weakness or timidity. It does not mean gentle. It does not mean "gentle and pleasant" or "patient, mild and soothing" or "flexible." Neither does it mean "too submissive" or "easily imposed on; spineless; spiritless."[1] These are all ways in which the word has been brought into our language. It has been misunderstood by more than one scholar. It was suggested by one that the use of this word "seems to be a slip,"[2] as if it is ill defined or ill placed and thus misunderstood to such a degree that either God or the oldest of manuscripts have made a mistake in its use! Here is the challenge: When the word *prautes* is brought into English as, for example, "meek," the current meaning of *meek* is applied to it. Wrong! And because the meaning of *meek* has morphed through time, it gets further and further from the true meaning of *prautes*—again, wrong! The same is true when it is translated as *gentle* or *humble* or any of the other words used. Don't get me wrong, these words are all good words and have meaning and merit—but not in the context of defining our word. As we will see, several of these words do come into consideration because they may be the result of our word but they do not define it. It is important to see that the essence of *prautes* is not an action or an attitude dependent on human will. It obviously involves our will, but because it is a work from on high, it is considerably deeper than just that. It simply is not an aspect solely of human definition or temperament.

All this begs the question: So just what is the real meaning, the substance, of prautes? It describes, and so is, a condition of the mind and heart that results in a particular overall perspective and subsequent lifestyle. Prautes is a state of mind while simultaneously being a condition of the heart. It is clearly a work of Holy Spirit in the inner man.

As Scripture defines Scripture, let's start there. In Matthew 11:29, referring to Jesus, there is the phrase "gentle of heart." The true definition of the word *gentle* lends much to our word. The King James Version translates it as "lowly in heart." That helps, yet it is far beyond just that. Lowly in heart would be one of the results of the action of the word. Jesus was "lowly in heart," but how is it that he came to this place? The word means "humiliated in circumstance or disposition; humility of mind; lowliness, even loneliness of mind."[3] Herein lies the beginning of insight into our word. To be "humiliated in circumstance" would be just that. One would have gone through many circumstances wherein humiliation would be experienced to arrive at "lowly in heart." It is interesting to note that humble, humility, and humiliation are all from the same root. Prautes is seen here and would come about as a result of this. Thus, to define the word as humble is quite incomplete and does not do it justice. It produces humility but does not mean simply humble.

The Old Testament defines and uses our word as "depressed, poor, needy, low, afflicted, rejected, oppressed and despised, while simultaneously meaning gentle, humble, quiet within."[4] On the surface, it seems to be meaning two different things. In its depth, what is truly being communicated is this: the first set of words describing *prautes*, when lived out, produces the second set of words. It does have a dual meaning. Moses was called "the most meek man" (Numbers 12:3). Jesus was called the same (Isaiah 53:7). There is our word in its original meaning. It seems each of them went through all of these things to come to prautes. All these words describe both the action taken to come to prautes and also the result therein. To be praus is to be broken, but not just. It is to be humbled, humiliated, brought down, by way of the first set of words, as many times as it takes for the will and determination of man to be yielded in totality to the will of the Father. It is in this way that one becomes defined by the second set of words: quiet, truly humble, gentle. Initially, this might sound horrible. And there are times when it may feel horrible—think of Jesus in Gethsemane. But remember from chapter 2 that "His ways are not our ways, but are far superior for a far superior purpose" and "the results are phenomenal!"

An intricate component of this word, this place of being, has all to do with obedience. As was stated earlier, Jesus learned obedience through suffering. It is the same for anyone who desires to live in this place of depth beyond measure. It is the willingness to obey, to respond to God with a yielded, obedient heart, that works *prautes* into the spirit of man. Holy Spirit brings life's troubles and struggles and difficulties to bear as often as is needed to produce the fruit of prautes. Moses is a good example. Jesus is the ultimate example. One can see this work clearly in Job, in Joseph and David, in Paul and Peter, in James and John, and more. In prautes, one can see the Father's work: molding and making the soul, the inner man into the person of God he intends. As was discussed partially in chapter 3, when Jesus says to "Deny yourself and take up your cross and follow me" (Matthew 16:24), this is what he is referring to. If one is to live this life as it was and is intended to be lived, according to the plan of the Creator, this is not optional—it is an act of obedience, and it is required, mandatory, imperative. The full text here says, "If anyone would come after me, he must deny himself and take up his cross and follow me. For whoever wants to save his life will lose it, but whoever loses his life for me will find it." It is clearer in the Amplified: "If anyone desires to be my disciple, let him deny himself [disregard, lose sight of, and forget himself and his own interests] and take up his cross and follow me [cleave steadfastly to me, conform wholly to my example].... For whoever is bent on saving his [temporal] life [his comfort and security here] shall lose ... [eternal life]; and whoever loses his life [his comfort and security here] for my sake shall find ... [life everlasting]."

This is a high calling and is not for the weak and feeble minded (Hebrews 12:12). As the text indicates, it will cost you everything. As the text indicates, it bears wonderful results on this side and the other. And as the text indicates, it is the true calling of all who would call on the name of Jesus as Savior and Lord. This is our charge.

So here it is: if there is a word that translates from the original *prautes* into English, it would be "tamed." And because the one tamed is no longer about or focused on self but always on the one taming, *prautes* is fully defined as "tamed by the Tamer."

[Selah]

Brown says, "It is the *opposite* of self-expression," and "It is in *contrast* to the attitude which demands its rights at all costs"[5] (emphasis mine). Oh, my, that is the antithesis of the heart of the global society in which we currently live! Jesus emulates prautes as "the one who is fixed wholly on God. [Through obedience] he was and is wholly submitted and yielded to his Father."[6] For us, this comes about when we are linked with Christ in spirit not just in understanding and are being fully conformed to his image.

Prautes is the grace of God blended and worked fully into the inner man. It is "that attitude of soul and spirit wherein we accept God's dealings with us as good and do not dispute or resist."[7]

This is another component of our word. Early on, as the Lord was working the reality of prautes well past my mind and into my heart, he said to me, "I'm bringing you to the place where you take no offense. Over anything. Or anyone. At any time. Ever." That is a very difficult and challenging place to be, and it does not come naturally. It does not come easily or quickly, not by any stretch of the imagination. But here it is: if he is truly Lord of my life, and if I am allowing him his rightful place there, then I am yielded fully to him. In that case, it is not about whatever the source of agitation or irritation or conflict might be. That source has been given over to him. Period. This comes by way of a death to said source, which is truly a death to me, to self. This is his work in me. When he has accomplished this, then what remains is a heart and a heart attitude that is his in me. Said another way, all that remains is him in me; what comes forth from me is him. Prautes.

What do you do when the guy cuts you off in traffic, or a woman stuffs herself in front of you into a space that is not safely there? What do you do when some act of injustice flairs up in your face? Yeah, me too, in the natural manner of living life. But see this: The one who is living prautes has been broken, has been trained and tamed by the Tamer to not respond in that manner. It is not a performance thing—far from it. It is a heart condition. It is a heart so transformed, so full of the love and presence of Jesus that it is at peace, in shalom. Continually. Constantly. Confidently.

Jesus *is* prautes. This is expressed clearly in that, again, he "became obedient [fully and completely, without hesitation, without indecision or qualm, without wavering or pause] through suffering" (Hebrews 5:8). He is our example for all of life. Philippians 2:3–8 captures it well: "Do nothing out of selfish ambition or vain conceit, … consider others better than yourselves. Your attitude should be the same as that of Christ Jesus: who …

made himself nothing, taking the very nature of a servant … he humbled himself and became obedient to death – even death on a cross." Can you begin to see that prautes is not simply humility or simply gentleness? It is much more complex than that.

To be praus is to carry a "quiet and friendly composure which does not become embittered or angry at what is unpleasant [or challenging]. This is an active attitude and deliberate acceptance, not just a passive submission. Greatness of soul [of character] is demonstrated by this superior acceptance."[8] It is "the humble and gentle attitude [and subsequent actions and behavior] which expresses itself in a patient [yieldedness] to offense; it is free from malice and desire for revenge."[9] One walking in and living out prautes will "acknowledge not their own will but the great and gracious will of God."[10] And yet it is more than a mere acknowledgment. It is to lay down all of one's own will and agenda, ideas, desires, plans, and patterns of life. It is to say no to self and yes to the will, directive, and command of Father on all fronts and on all occasions.

[Selah]

This is no easy road. "This temper is first of all toward God but is also toward men, even evil men, out of a sense that these, with the insults and injuries which they may inflict, are permitted and [even] employed by him for the chastening and purifying of his elect, his people."[11] The praus person "surrenders everything to the Lord and His control. He bears injustice patiently and without bitterness."[12] The natural man does not readily tend toward or yield to the things of God. By nature, we are much too selfish for that. We want our comfort, our way. In all honesty, it is still fairly easy for me to be all about me! Ugh! Even after all these years with the Lord, sometimes I can quickly default to self and the weak ways of same. It is no easy road. To borrow from Jesus's disciples in John 6:60, "This is a hard teaching, who can accept it?" But a few verses later, verse 68, Peter says, "Lord, to whom shall we go? You [alone] have the words of eternal life." The bottom line is there are many who do not walk through the small and narrow gate, and few who do. (Matthew 7:13–14) Yet in these times, the call is intense, and many will make this choice.

What we are talking about here is the stark difference between Jesus as Savior and Jesus as Lord. Now well into the twenty-first century, the tangible reality of the latter has become quite rare. I don't say this to criticize; it is simply an observation. The biblical mandate to lordship has fallen far away within the social and spiritual pressures and subsequent choices of most. The call is nothing new; it is first found in the garden. The tension, the conflict within the heart of man over this, is nothing new either; it is also first found in the garden (Genesis 3–4). Through the ages, men and women have struggled with just who is on the throne of their lives. Today the options are many. Couple this with the high price of discipleship and death to self, and the current results are almost to be expected.

One more thought to close this chapter (we will pick this up again later). As seen in the life of Jesus, there is a direct connection between prautes and the helplessness found in chapter 3. Jesus, because of his total voluntary yielding to Father, had no means of enforcing his rights and ultimately had to suffer all manner of injustice; he was helpless. Jesus also walked in all things praus. For us, the helplessness brings us to that place of understanding in the heart exactly who and what we *are not* in our own strength. We see our weaknesses and sin nature. Prautes clearly spells out who and what we *are* in Christ. The applied truth of helplessness is to see that this life is all about God; he is God and we are not. In love he created us to be with him on his terms. The applied truth of prautes fully embraces this, and from there brings us to the tangible reality of who we are in him, with all the value and purpose, the presence and depth, and the power and authority he brings. When I have died to my self long enough for it to be now a lifestyle; when I have so yielded to the Lord that I don't matter anymore, only he and his ways matter; when he is truly my all in all and I am perfectly content to simply be, that is prautes.

Chapter 6

Prautes, Part Two

Matthew 5:5 states, "Bless-ed are the meek, for they will inherit the earth."

In 1998, Robert Redford and Kristin Scott Thomas starred in a movie called *The Horse Whisperer.* Great movie. As is the case in most movies, it is a mixture of things moral and things not. The storyline, like the acting, is very strong and intriguing, and there are several subplots that keep one paying close attention. I mention it here because if one sees the story through the eyes of the horse, it strikes a chord with prautes. I'll resist the temptation to tell the whole story!

The horse (let's call him Stallion) and rider (played by a young Scarlett Johansson) get in a tragic accident where both are seriously injured and close to death. The decision is made to save the horse, and it heals but becomes very aggressive and unmanageable. The girl is physically damaged for life and has profound emotional struggles. They take Stallion across country to a man (Robert Redford) who can help. He takes them on and, through his rules, methods, and procedures, brings the horse back to a place of health and stability. That is really abbreviated!

What is of interest is the progression of the horse's persona through the course of events. The accident has left him extremely fearful; his rage and aggression are a direct result. He is truly uncontrollable. In her own way, so is the girl. At first Redford simply allows Stallion to be on his own; there are people and other animals around at a distance. Over time he engages the horse and a relationship ensues. With continued interaction, Stallion comes to trust Redford. It is then that the story gains intrigue. As the trust grows, he puts the horse through a series of events that stretch, and subsequently build and fortify, that trust. Finally, at the apex of the movie, he has the horse in a corral and is working with him. He then hobbles the horse (ties one of the forelegs up so the horse must manage on three legs). Stallion is now at a point where he can do nothing and is helpless, but he has been drawn into this state within the context of trust. Redford then backs Stallion down to a kneeling position while he does the same; horse and trainer are as close to one another as possible. Stallion is broken and has no more fear, no more aggression. He is at full and complete peace and trust with his trainer and with himself. This scene makes me cry.

Friend, this is prautes. This is the all-knowing wise and gentle hand and heart of the Tamer entering into the ugly, horrific, damaged world of one of his creation. This is the Tamer walking alongside his precious ones, working with them in the midst of their fear and pain, uncertainty and darkness, and bringing them to that place of wholeness. Together. Redford kneeled with Stallion. He came into Stallion's world and walked with him through to total healing. It was all in an environment of developed trust, within the atmosphere of safety, security, and unconditional love. Stallion is you and me. (That does not make Redford God!) What the Father wants to build is a relationship so deep, so rich and real, that we will follow his lead and walk with him in and under any and all of life's situations and circumstances. Together.

Tamed. Broken by the Tamer; made to see our helplessness; made helpless. Redford had to break the horse to break its pride, rage, and anger—its inner-man issues, if you will. (I said this earlier, but apparently it bears repeating: as important as it seems, it matters not from where these issues came; it matters only that they are broken and thus removed.) Built by the Tamer; brought to prautes. Built to a place of total peace with him and with self to a place of total yieldedness, which produces an amazing confidence in the Tamer (and if seen correctly, in self as well) and in the relationship with him. In confidence, strength, and power, every bit as strong as before the whole ordeal, Stallion will now do whatever it is that Redford directs him to in trust and without even an inkling of doubt or hesitation, knowing full well there are no maneuverings or ulterior motives in the heart of the trainer. With brokenness now complete, healing is now whole. The trainer has built a trust, a mutual trust, that is all-inclusive and non-negotiable. Period. Beyond the illustration and into the reality here being defined, this is intimacy beyond measure—certainly beyond human measure. No matter what, no matter when, and no matter how or why, my soul and my spirit is at peace, at one with my Maker, my Tamer. Yours can be too if you will allow him his work in you. Amazingly wonderful. Wonderfully amazing.

[Selah]

So as to not leave you hanging, the rest of the movie is beautiful. Stallion, now restored, is reintroduced to the girl, and together they reunite, grow strong, and, as is the way with all good movies, live happily ever after!

The manner in which the Lord develops prautes runs against the grain of our understanding; we basically do not have a grid for it. In the movie, Redford works Stallion through a series of events that stretch but also build and fortify trust. For us, these are the many hard and difficult things the Father is pleased to bring us through. Most often he does not need to create these struggles; they are simply a part of life, simply the fallen nature of man. At other times, he does set things in motion to build that deeper character. This is seen clearly in Job, where Yahweh directs Lucifer's attention toward Job. It is described as well in Hebrews 12:5–13 and James 1:2–15 regarding us believers. Jesus' work with Peter is quite revelatory here. Luke 22:31 says, "Simon, Simon, [Simon Peter] behold, Satan has demanded permission to sift you as wheat; but I have prayed for you, that your faith may not fail; and you, when once you have turned [back] again, strengthen your brothers" (NASB).

This is a personal vendetta! Satan is out to get him. This is the only time in the New Testament that the word *sift* is used. It means to riddle, to sift through a sieve. It is to make holes in, to puncture throughout. So it is this: "Satan is going to poke holes through you (your heart and mind), through your faith, until you are punctured throughout, until you look and feel like a sieve." From our perspective, the horrible part is that Jesus does not stop him! Instead he says, "But I have prayed for you that your faith [heart, life] won't totally drain out [out of the bucket full of holes that is to be your life]. And when you are restored that you will be able to strengthen the brethren."

Jesus, why would you do that? On the surface it seems not just hard but wrong, even cruel. In truth, seen in its entirety, it is not. This is what it takes to bring Peter into that place the Father desires and has for him to be, so as to be in total alignment and agreement, total harmony with him, and thus with the call and purpose on his life. This action produced in Peter the full and complete man of God by way of the full and complete sacrificial yieldedness unto God, poured out before the throne. All of this is the dual nature of prautes, the intense struggle and difficulty on the front side and the amazing personal relational depth and richness as a result.

If we are paying attention, we can see the Lord is always pouring and emptying for this very intention. If we fail to see the purpose, we get frustrated and confused; we lose hope and vision. We must understand that all of this is the ceaseless dealings of God in building us to prautes. It has been said this way: "God's activity upon us is the guarantee of the value he places in us, and of the ultimate intensions he has for us."[1]

One who is praus is one who is walking in a most far-reaching brokenness with a deep and thoroughly tender heart. This results in a tamed and tempered spirit, a Spirit-controlled spirit affecting, leading, and guiding our whole being. One who is praus understands completely the sovereignty of God, and so the reality of God's hand and control in all things, without debate, dissent, or resistance. This person is fully sensitized to Holy Spirit and to his voice, urgings, and promptings. He or she is fully tenderized by the love of the Father, which subsequently produces a richer love for the Father, and they live together accordingly. One living here is walking in a confidence that is genuine and comes not from self but from God. It is that place of rarity, rich and whole. It comes with a presence and resulting power, always his, that is immeasurable and completely unattainable any other way.

I want that. How about you?

We often see the hand of God as David expressed. Psalms 6:2–3 says, "Oh Lord, heal me, for my bones are in agony; my soul is in anguish. How long, Lord, how long?" Psalms 13:1–2 says, "How long, oh Lord? Will you forget me forever? How long will you hide your face from me? How long must I wrestle with my thoughts and every day have sorrow in my heart? How long will my enemy triumph over me?" And then he cried out in Psalms 10:1, "Why, oh Lord, do you stand far off? Why do you hide yourself in times of trouble?" And again in Psalms 22:1, "My God, my God, why have you forsaken me? Why are you so far from saving me, so far from the words of my groaning?"

This is David's cry, and it is ours as well. It is the cry of our humanity in its pain and suffering, but also in its shortsightedness. This is our lament that comes because we do not see his ways and means of working to build his loved ones, his creation. I once asked him the same question as David: "How long, Lord?" His reply was clear enough. "As long as it takes to break you, tame you, restore you, and empower you." Well! That both hurt me deeply and encouraged me greatly! What a mystery this God of ours can be sometimes!

The truth is that he has not and does not forsake us (Psalm 37:25). Although it does feel that way mostly because of his silence, it is not so. The Father said to me once, "Do you realize that my silence is most often my vote of confidence in you? I have you just where I want you, and you are doing well." That was a very surprising revelation—and quite soothing to my sour soul! There is a silence. There is a quietness, a seeming distance. It is by design. He has not left or forsaken us, or turned his back on us. It is the work of prautes. It is but a season in the process of sanctification generally, and prautes specifically.

We see it as struggle and hardship. But he sees it as this: the prautes manifested by Jesus, and commended to the believer, is actually the fruit of power. One of the fruits of the Spirit, in Galatians 5:22–23, is "gentleness." The word there is our word. And when one has endured and learned to live the life of prautes, one walks with the Most High in intimacy—and subsequently in his power. Here, presence and power are one. The common assumption is that when a man is meek, it is because he is weak and cannot help himself. But Jesus was meek and because of that had "the infinite resources of God at his sway."[2] This came as a result of the brokenness that ushered in prautes. Our word is the antitheses of self-assertiveness and self-interest. It is equanimity of spirit. Equanimity implies an inherent evenness of temper that is not easily disturbed but rather is composed. It is neither elated nor cast down because it is not occupied with self and its surroundings at all. Prautes is a condition of the mind and heart that walks in and so demonstrates this equanimity; in gentleness, not in weakness but in power. It develops into and so is a virtue born in strength of character. All brought on by the hand and heart of our loving Father.

We will pick this up in fullness in chapter 11, but I want to share this quote with you here because it captures prautes so well. It comes from Andy Park, a Vineyard pastor and worship leader. I found it on a Vineyard CD jacket, though which one I'm not sure.

> God is raising up an army for the last days. It will not be, however, an army that will fight with "the weapons of this world"—that is, personally wielding power on God's behalf. Instead this army will battle in a seemingly foolish way: by simply walking in humble submission before God, listening to his voice and explicitly obeying it. The people of this army will be characterized by great

> faith tempered with depth of humility. [There it is: great faith involves the action of having been tempered, tamed.] Their faith will be unshakeable yet not arrogant, for their confidence will not be in their own gifting but in God's faithfulness. Their humility will not be apologetic for while they will understand their weakness they will be intimately related to his strength. [There it is again!] They will be people under authority. When this army is raised the very gates of hell will tremble for it will be a sign that the King is ready to establish his Kingdom "on earth as it is in heaven."

I'm not sure, but I am guesstimating the quote to be over twenty years old. And here we are, living right in the midst of it …

In closing this chapter, I want to reiterate a bit. Walking entirely in the world of prautes brings several factors to play in mind and heart, in life and lifestyle. There is a significantly deeper place of trust and rest and peace; one is much closer to the Lord and hears from him much more readily. One no longer is compelled to ask the "Why?" question; it simply is not a factor. One is totally focused on the Lord and not at all on the circumstances of life; they are in his hands. Instead, one learns to ask the right questions: What are you doing? What are you wanting to accomplish in me, in my heart at this time? What are you wanting me to do with this present heart circumstance and condition? Who are you wanting me to be here? Who are you developing me into here? It is essential to see in this the joy found and described in James 1:2–4, where the author is speaking to the value of this work. This is very difficult, no doubt. It can be and often is slow and long, agonizing and distressing, often to the place of seeming excruciation. For Jesus, it came to the point of actually sweating blood (Luke 22:44). We have not yet arrived at that point (Hebrews 12:4). We do well to see this as it is intended, to see the big picture and the purposes behind it all. Paul capsulizes it with excellence in Philippians 4:11–12 when he says, "I have learned to be content whatever the circumstances. … I have learned the secret of being content." He learned; it did not come naturally or easily. Content here is not complacent; it is not apathetic or lethargic. It is not the prevailing attitude of the day reflected in the word *whatever.* No. It is much closer to *shalom*, which is a peace that is all-encompassing. When one is living fully in shalom, all that is within and without them is at peace; it is an overriding, overwhelming peace that has effect on all and in all. Going back to Stallion in the story of *The Horse Whisperer,* he came to the place, and he was tamed to the place wherein he was completely contented—in the stall, in the pasture, at rest, at play, and in service to and with his master.

Bless-ed are the tamed, those tamed by the Tamer, those walking and living in the deepest places of trust and confidence in and with their Lord. Bless-ed are those who live in the God-given harmony of presence and power, all from and for the One. Prautes. Let's go there …

Chapter 7

Those Who Hunger and Thirst for Righteousness

Matthew 5:6 says, "Bless-ed are those who hunger and thirst for righteousness, for they will be filled."

My wife and I had the privilege and joy of sitting on a Hawaiian beach for a few days several years ago. It was a delightful time. One day we spent the whole day on the sand, in the sun, and under an umbrella, taking in a marvelous fragment of God's creation. If time and money were not an issue … I'll let you finish the sentence!

During this day, I had an opportunity to observe human nature and behavior in a very distinct yet all-too-common manner. About midmorning, a family of four arrived on the scene: Mom,

Dad, and two children around ten and twelve years old. The two children, brother and sister, had boogie boards in their arms and glee in their eyes. Down to the water they ran, very excited to try out their new toys in the amazing ocean expanse that offered itself to them. Mom and Dad settled in on the sand. It only took a few minutes, and Dad was on his cell phone while Mom was buried in a romance novel. Can you see where this is going? Boogie boards look easy on TV, but there is technique required; there is a learning curve. Susie and Johnny were trying hard—they were all in. They had no clue what they were doing or even what they were supposed to be doing. They were looking up at Mom and Dad for support, but there was none. They were left all alone. Soon the energy and excitement of a new adventure turned sour. Disappointment. Discouragement. Frustration. And then little Johnny got angry and started acting up. Dad scooped up all the gear, Mom grabbed the children, and down the road they went.

A while later, here came another family: Mom, Dad, and three boys, probably eight, ten, and eleven. Those boys also had boogie boards in their arms and were well past glee and full on into pure glory in their eyes! It was obvious to me that they had been primed for this adventure and were like kids in a candy store with the hearty approval of Mom to eat all they could! Dad took the time to help Mom set up camp on the sand, and then he raced down to the water with the boys! He got in the water with them and very intentionally spent time with each one to teach them the basic technique required to manage their boards. Only when he was satisfied that all three of them were comfortable with their boards did he look up at Mom, make eye contact, and return to her side. From there, the two of them engaged one another while watching and enjoying their sons frolicking in that vast ocean expanse, thrilled to the bone. They stayed for hours.

Perhaps I am sharing this with you because it is so impacting to me, because of my own childhood experiences. I can relate very closely with little Johnny, and my sisters can relate with Susie. Or perhaps it is the raw, unadulterated rage that often wells up within me when I witness or experience injustice on any level. Either way, albeit subtle and seemingly insignificant, this story is reflective of the selfish, inappropriate, hurtful, unjust actions that surround us all. When this injustice becomes magnified over the earth, it is almost overwhelming. Bringing it closer to home, when this injustice is sensed and seen, it stirs us to take action, it makes us cry out for what is right, and it makes us hungry.

The wolf who has not eaten for a day is hungry. The wolf who has not eaten for two weeks is hungry. It is the same word—hungry. The word in the second sentence carries considerably more weight, impact, and significance than it does in the first.

This contrast illustrates our word hunger; it is not a casual word. It is to desire strongly,[1] but it's more. The word is to famish.[2] It expresses a fervent longing, an obsession for something one cannot live without.[3] The longer the wolf goes without food, the more he is pained with hunger, and the more intense is his cry, his need, for sustenance. The hungrier the wolf becomes, the stronger his necessity. It becomes a driving force; it becomes his sole and entire focus. This is the intensity of our word hunger, except it has nothing to do with food. Bless-ed are those who need in their hunger for righteousness. There is a sense of craving, of fervent yearning. It is not just to desire strongly—it is to strongly and passionately desire.[4]

The desire is not for anything of self, of the natural man; it is not a personal righteousness,[5] but for the righteousness of the Righteous One.

The hungry are men who [are] both outwardly and inwardly painfully deficient in the things essential to life as God meant it to be, and who, since they cannot help themselves, turn to God on the basis of his promises. These men, and these alone, find God's help in Jesus. The hungry who are bless-ed are not beggars. They are believers who seek help from Jesus because of [the keen awareness of] their own helplessness [and that of those around them]. This hunger is not [merely] a concern or striving for uprightness; it is the desire, fed by painful lack, that God's will be done.[6]

It is understood here, without need for qualification or definition, that God's will is right.

The meaning of thirst is in a similar vein. The parched palate, the desiccated throat, the joints and flesh that hurt from dehydration—this defines thirst in our context. To crave water, to be ravenous for whatever will quench—this is our word. It is as stated in Psalm 63:1, "My soul thirsts for you, my body longs for you, in a dry and weary land where there is no water." And in Isaiah 26:9 it says, "My soul yearns for you in the night; in the morning my spirit longs for you."

Together, these two words "mutually reinforce the meaning of great [and intense] desire [and need]. They also carry the implication of an existing lack."[7] The wolf with belly full does not drive for food, for satisfaction. He is not hungry; there is no lack. As with the verb *mourn* in chapter 4, those so hungering and thirsting truly are pining, which is to have an intense longing, an agonizing, for the righteousness of the Lord with an ongoing, continuous pursuit.

Righteousness in this passage carries the same intensity and magnitude as do hunger and thirst. In this context, the word would most accurately be translated as "the righteous" or "the just." It is in the Greek that way for importance, the article *the* bringing that emphasis. But it is not directly referring to people or actions that are righteous. Righteousness is the state or condition commanded by God. Righteousness is God's rightness or uprightness assigned to humanity. Perhaps it can best be seen as the claim which he has upon man. On one hand it is a gift (Romans 5:17), while on the other hand it is a command and the standard of life in him. It is righteousness that is that right and true thing that comes from the Righteous One. It is "the act of doing what God requires; doing what is right [according to him]."[8] It is "the right conduct of man, which follows the will of God." It "brings the disciple into harmony with the will of God."[9] And it brings about "behavior which is in keeping with the two-way relationship between God and man."[10]

These definitions are all right and accurate, but there is more. There is a deeper dynamic going on here. This hunger and thirst has to do much more with the cry for and condition of the inner man and all of the consequential issues we find in this life. Certainly, it includes outward behavior, actions, and reactions, but here it has more to do with the heart, with the heart's current state and its subsequent connection with the Lord (or lack thereof), from which will flow the outward behavior. As Jesus is the Righteous One (1 John 2:1) and we believers are the righteousness of Christ, (Philippians 1:11; 3:9), in this context, that is what is being focused on and cried out for. Those who hunger and thirst do so seeking that which is from him, from his righteous state or place—not as man might define or understand, but as he is. Here, righteousness is an all-encompassing thing. Theologically it would be identified as "the inherent rectitude of the divine nature,"[11] rectitude meaning rightness. Jesus speaks directly to this in John 17:25 when he calls his Father "Righteous Father." When Righteous

Father is on the scene and is invited into the mix, things change; they become as he is. That is what is being sought. That is what is being ached and yearned for.

This need actually goes past righteousness. It goes to one of the main results of a righteousness manifested: justice.

Might the tangible result of righteousness in fact be justice? If all of us collectively were living in this defined state of righteousness, would we not be living in a state of justice, of things just? How could it be otherwise? It is interesting that the two words share much in their respective definitions. If things are righteous, they are right. If things are just, they are correct. *Right* and *correct* can mean the exact same thing, depending upon context. In the Greek New Testament, as a noun or verb, the root word for *rightness* is used about 60 percent of the time as *righteousness* and over 30 percent of the time as *justice*. They are, if not twins, certainly very close brothers. I would suggest that the one actually breeds the other.

Those who so readily sense injustice, those who have been the recipients of unjust actions, and those who ache accordingly know full well of wrong and incorrect. That is why they so ache for the opposite. The more one has experienced wrong, the more the soul cries, aches, for wrong to be righted. That is the definition; that is the action of justice. (We will see this more clearly in chapter 10: the action of justice finds is roots in prautes.)

It would be good to note, understand, and embrace that no one has more experienced this injustice than Jesus himself. Study him and his life, and you will see the accuracy of this statement. No wonder he is known as the Just or the Just One (Acts 3:14, 7:52, 22:14 KJV), because he has such an affinity for what is just based in part from his experiences as a man with what was unjust.

Righteousness is brother to justice, and justice is what is right. In the context of this Beatitude, I propose the creation of a new verb form, "to just," which is to right wrong. This would better fit the heart of the matter. Aligned with the heart and intention of the Author of justice, "to just" is to expend whatever righteous energy is required, in whatever manner is righteously appropriate, in order to bring into right standing something or someone, that is skewed, twisted, or maligned in thought, deed, or action, no matter the source, man, beast, or devil. The end game of "to just" is to bring truth to the lie no matter its source or root, and to affect it to change—not partial but full and complete change. It might be that "to justify," which is "to show to be right, to vindicate," would fit here, but that does not express the fullness of it. The word *justify* answers the question "What?" in the context of its use. But "to just" is not simply answering a question because that may or may not actually bring conclusion. To just is to solve or resolve the dilemma, the problem. It is bringing closure, a finality to that problem. The dictionary would classify *just* as an adjective. Okay. I am saying, in the context of the depth of this Beatitude, that it would be a participle, which, if you remember from Kevin's coffee pushing (chapter 2), is a noun given the place of a verb, given a place of action for emphasis. It is this action that captures the heart of hungering and thirsting. However it is construed, justice is an entity of action toward rightness and is brother to righteousness.

It is not just me on a warm, sunny beach struggling with unfairness. We are all wired to sense justice and injustice; it is in our bones. Just ask the little boy who had his sucker or his cookie stolen by the bully. He lost his cookie, yes. But perhaps the bigger thing with him isn't the loss of some sweetness but the injustice of being used, of being taken advantage of, of being assaulted or abused in some manner, of being subjected to something unjust. This is what screams in the soul. Remembering that these Beatitudes are character traits of Jesus, this is what screams in his soul.

Those who hunger and thirst here are coming from the vantage point of that little boy but on a much larger scale. It is not the sucker, and it is not even personal, although it can be by relating to the bigger picture. It is the rejection or the snub, the being ignored or overlooked. It is the person, the people group, and even the nation being leveraged for someone else's gain. It is not the cookie; it is human trafficking, it is rape or murder, it is genocide. It is the racial slur that was so out of line and unfair no matter the color, no matter the continent. There are so many examples. It is the continued unjust act or worldview behind the act that goes on and on seemingly without end. It is our sin and sin nature as humans that continue to breed and propagate wrong and evil. It is the relentless angst, the oft-repeated sorrow and trouble in the soul over things iniquitous and heinous in our world. The cry is from the very bottom of the very essence of right versus wrong. Perhaps it's better emphasized as wrong versus right. We see the wrong fighting right. We cry out and yearn to see the right fighting wrong.

This becomes all the more heightened in light of the reality of the Cross, of the taste of justice served. Jesus died for the injustices in this world. The Just One came to die and in that restored what was first intended. He put into motion the action of justice that will one day come to full fruition. Now seeing, now having been made aware, now having tasted of that and of what is right and just in the world, we want it all to be that way. And because it is not yet in that place, we see and sense the gap. Therefore we hunger and thirst.

Jesus died for injustice. He lives for justice. His righteousness brings justice. We are the righteousness of Christ if we are walking with him (Romans 4:5; 2 Corinthians 5:21). He would have us take on his personality, his character traits, and travel with him through the course of this life and on to the next, living as he lives. In this case, that is fighting for right. This is the call, with this understanding: If you desire to go ever deeper with God, which is also his desire, you will never stop mourning, hungering, and thirsting in your ache and yearning for more of him and of his Kingdom manifested.

Bless-ed are those who ache, who crave, and who yearn in their need for the righteousness of the Right One to be seen, to be on the scene, so as to bring justice to the table.

There is a note of caution needed here. We must be careful to avoid the temptation to vengeance. Most often, those who can personally relate to the injustices of this life have reason to hunger and thirst for his justice and righteousness to show up on the scene. That would be the scene of injustice and unrighteousness, which these same people (present company included) have so experienced. The natural man wants justice, certainly, but often because of the wound and the hurt that come from that injustice, that desire for justice comes with the tainted heart of vengeance. It is easy to feel as though vengeance is required and thus justified or rationalized. In our humanity, this need for vengeance can take us so far as to seethe, to rage for it. Here, vengeance is to get even. The heart of this word speaks to retaliation or revenge, even violent revenge. There is the clear element of bitterness and hatefulness found here. To yield to this temptation is not to walk as Jesus walked. If measured by the ways of the natural man, there is no one who has more right to vengeance than Jesus. Yet he exercised none. To the contrary, as we have seen in chapters 3, 5, and 6 with the reality of helplessness and prautes, Jesus simply yielded, deferring his own heart, his own sense of and need for justice to the Father. He broke in his injury, harm, and humiliation, and he broke toward his Lord—always. We are called to follow suit.

Chapter 8

Coalescence

Matthew 5:3–6 says, "Bless-ed are the poor in spirit, for theirs is the kingdom of heaven. Bless-ed are those who mourn, for they will be comforted. Bless-ed are the meek, for they will inherit the earth. Bless-ed are those who hunger and thirst for righteousness, for they will be filled."

This chapter is intended to pull together the first four Beatitudes, first from what they establish and then from what they promise.

From chapter 1:

> The Beatitudes are progressive, each building on the preceding in the genius that can only come from the Author. Though they can each stand alone, when placed together there is a unity, even

> a community, among them. As they are placed together, they gain in strength, the sum being more than the total of the parts. It is nothing less than sheer brilliance, the manner in which the Author has designed and constructed all of his Word; it's no more evident than within this section of Scripture. The first four weave and build an amazing spiritual reality, clearly reflecting the character of Jesus, working together to create a phenomenal base.

If we are going past an intellectual understanding; if we are entering into what was previously communicated (see the notes at the end of chapter 4), going to epignosis and not just gnosis; if we are actually experientially engaging Jesus, his character, and his heart and allowing Holy Spirit to do his job, to teach and train us, to change us into the likeness of the Triune God; then we are well on our way to a new life, to the life he wants with us and has intended for us all along. From that statement, capture the reality of what is behind the thoughts here. If we have said yes to Jesus, we are bless-ed, and we are favored, honored, and highly esteemed by God. This statement is fully and totally true, whether or not it seems or feels that way. It is true because it comes from the One who is always true. "God is not a man that he should lie, nor a son of man that he should change his mind. Does he speak and then not act? Does he promise and then not fulfill?" (Numbers 23:19). We do well to recognize that the "seems likes" and the "feels likes" of life are not always things to be relied upon. They fall into the realm of feelings, of emotion, which in and of themselves can be fickle at best, suspect often, and incorrect much of the time!

Someone, somewhere said, "Don't ever make a serious decision or determination from an emotional state." That is a very accurate statement. All too often we measure and weigh life, its situations and circumstances, from this place of emotion, from how whatever is happening makes us feel. This is by default a place of subjectiveness—as opposed to objectiveness. It is, or certainly can be, a place of uncertainty, and often there's irrationality as opposed to rationality. It can come from a place of fear and insecurity with all of the subsequent senses, sentiments, and responses that follow. Don't get me wrong; I am not here slamming emotion or emotions. I am one of the more emotional men I know. The God I know and love is quite emotional himself! I am simply pointing out that when it comes to weighing, measuring, and assessing God and the truth he is, brings, and walks in, it is not accurately done by means of emotion. What he says and how it feels to us are often not very close together. I choose to default to the former because I know from experience that the latter is not reliable, whereas the former is always and ever so. I said all that to say this: It is true that we are the privileged recipients of divine favor.

Taking that forward, there is some indication that the original order of things within the first four Beatitudes might have been slightly different than what is now seen. Some would indicate that the second and third Beatitude were originally reversed. "It is possible that the third originally followed the first, which is called synonymous parallelism, and that Matthew broke that [connection] with mourn [the second] to follow the lead of Isaiah 61:1–2."[1] In the end it matters not, but for the sake of discussion, making this shift perhaps helps us grasp things at a slightly deeper level.

Although it is clear that all the Beatitudes can be independent of one another, we have seen that there is a direct correlation between those helpless and those praus (see chapter 5). This shifts the thrust of the second half of these verses.

> Matthew 5:3: "helpless … for theirs is the Kingdom of heaven."

> Matthew 5:5: "tamed … for they will inherit the earth."
>
> Matthew 5:4: "mourning … for they will be comforted."
>
> Matthew 5:6: "hungering and thirsting … for they will be filled."

They then read this way: favored, honored, and highly esteemed are the ones helpless, the ones tamed, those mourning, hungering, and thirsting. Theirs is the Kingdom of heaven. They will be given the earth. They will be comforted. They will be filled and fully satisfied. When put together in that manner, it becomes a very powerful little paragraph!

Let's break this down. First with verses 3 and 5, helpless and tamed, and then with verses 4 and 6, mourning, hungering, and thirsting.

That verses 3 and 5 are closely connected is evidenced by way of their respective definitions and subsequent applications. Based on what has already been established (see the end of chapter 4), it is reasonable to say that one cannot come to the fullness of prautes except through the reality of helplessness. Said another way, one cannot come to the fullness of who they are in Christ without the stark reality of who they are not. Thus, it is in helplessness that the one tamed by the Tamer comes to completeness; in that sense, these two are tied together.

Bless-ed are those who have come to understand fully their helplessness, which is proof of who they are not in their own strengths and abilities, and is also proof of who God is. Bless-ed are those who have come to experientially and fully understand the reality of prautes, of who they truly are in light of full dependency on God, while having been thoroughly tamed by the Tamer. These people have come face-to-face with who they are not so that they can be brought heart to heart with who they are. They have the Kingdom, they own it. They will have the Earth, they will own it. For the sake of understanding, because the promises of God are "yes" and "amen" in Christ (2 Corinthians 1:20), which means they have and will come to fruition, we can bring the future tense into the present. Thus, this text can be rendered: "These people have the Kingdom and these people have the earth."

This is further supported by the grammar. The "will be" verbs in the Beatitudes are in the future passive voice. The future part of this designation does speak to a future event, but exactly when is not expressed. There are three forms of action, and two are of concern in this context: the active voice and the passive voice. Active means that whatever action is taken will come from the subject, such as "I will hear" or "I will give." Passive means the action of the verb is being done to the subject, such as "I am being heard" or "I will receive." This type of sentence structure is most often how phrases and sentences that are interpersonal in nature are constructed. Here is the point: because the word is passive, that means the action of "will be" is received by the subject (us) and is being accomplished by another (God in his sovereignty). It is then a given that we will inherit and be filled. The question is, exactly when is that point in time? Is it well into the future? Or is it more immediately following the encounter, as in just after mourning comes the comfort? I believe the answer is yes! It can be either, depending on the circumstances and what the Lord is intending to accomplish in the heart. Either way, we have been given nothing less than the Kingdom of God and his Earth! Wow. Think on that for a moment.

To add even more amazingness to this, in light of the tamed inheriting the earth, generally "to inherit" is to come into possession of, to become heir to, to take legal ownership of. An heir is one who inherits, one who has the right to own what has been bequeathed to them by the previous owner—in this case, none less than the Creator of it all. More specifically, in light of God's heart and intent, I would suggest that this inheritance does not mean that God is giving up ownership. To the contrary, "the idea of inheritance in the Bible is a reminder that God has not intended man to lead an autonomous, isolated, self-sufficient existence."[2] What is inherited not only comes from God but is God! It becomes a type of co-ownership, a relational interchange, a covenant, really, wherein we come alongside God to be and work together within Kingdom dynamics and Kingdom life. It is amazing to me that God loves you and me that much. Let's go spend a million dollars on a Lamborghini, or some such expression of wealth, and then simply give it away to the young son or daughter who has no clue of its value, simply because we love them and want to bless them and pour out from that love. Did you ever think of things that way? God loves you so very much because he wants to, and in this context, his demonstration of that love is supreme, extreme, and beyond comparison.

[Selah]

The power and significance we just discovered in verses 3 and 5 set up the following two verses. Within the "who we are not/who we are" truth and actuality, we are now fully in our place in Christ. There we are comforted; there we are filled. Bless-ed are those who mourn, who ache and grieve over injustices, as well as those who hunger and thirst, who are famished and craving for the righteousness of God. These people will be comforted; they will be filled.

To be comforted is to be exhorted in the way of consolation; that is to say, to be urged, to be highly admonished into the receiving of comfort, of strong encouragement. Said another way, to be exhorted is to be encouraged with a kick or, if you prefer, a nudge. In our context, because God is the comforter, (Jeremiah 8:18; John 14:16), it is to invoke God, to call him near, to invite him in. The word literally means "to call to the side of." It is us doing the calling and him responding, the net result of which is to have God by your side comforting as only he can do.

There is a bit of a caveat here. In the overall context of what the Lord is saying within the Beatitudes and then within the whole of Scripture, it is important to understand that although God is truly the God of comfort and is continually offering such to his own, he does not want us comfortable! We are on a journey. We are in the midst of one adventure after another. If we are listening and responding, we see that he has us on the move way more than at rest. By design, these points of action do not leave us comfortable!

I was invited into a group once to flow prophetically and to bring some insight, a fresh word, and some new direction, the Lord willing. The Lord was willing and had something to say, and we all left that time together with a number of nuggets, perhaps the most impactful being this: "Walk in the revelation, knowledge, and understanding that you are child to the King, brother to the Christ, and your personal trainer is Holy Spirit."

It is he, it is Holy Spirit, who is not willing to see us comfortable! He, the Comforter (John 14:16 KJV), will see to it that we are continually being stretched. I don't know about you, but my experiences with a personal trainer have often been painful as he pushes me forward well beyond my comfort zone and into new places of strength and endurance. Holy Spirit is doing a similar thing on a spiritual level.

To be filled is to be satisfied. It is an interesting word play because it is actually "to cause to eat one's fill so as to be satisfied, so as to want no more."[3] To be hungering is to be yearning, aching for truth, for justice and rightness to prevail. To be filled, then, is to be filled with the satisfaction that God rules and reigns in his faithfulness and has prevailed. To hunger is to want, to desire; to be fulfilled is to want no more, to desire no more because the want has been met. Remember the want of God and the will of God in the Introduction? Here, those who have hungered hunger no more because their want and their will have been met by his. This God of ours is so amazing! Justice will prevail. Where you and yours have been the subject of injustice and have been wronged, God in his faithfulness will bring right, will bring justice at some point in time, at his right time (Romans 5:18–19, 8:3b, 8:28a).

Again, favored, honored, and highly esteemed are the ones helpless, the ones tamed, those mourning, hungering, and thirsting. Theirs is the Kingdom of heaven. Theirs is the earth. In the timing of the Lord, they are being comforted, and they are being filled and fully satisfied.

Are you beginning to see the truth in what was previously stated in chapter 2? "The Beatitudes, fully engaged and applied, bring adventure and immense joy."

Chapter 9

The Merciful, the Pure, the Peacemakers

Matthew 5:7–9 declares, "Bless-ed are the merciful, for they will be shown mercy. Bless-ed are the pure in heart, for they will see God. Bless-ed are the peacemakers, for they will be called sons of God."

There is a passage in Timothy, and a particular word, that reflects well the intensity of the heart of Jesus within these three Beatitudes. First Timothy 6:11–15a says,

> But you, man of God, flee from all this, and pursue righteousness, *godliness*, faith, love, endurance and gentleness. Fight the good fight of faith. Take hold of the eternal life to which you

> were called when you made your good confession in the presence of many witnesses. In the sight of God, who gives life to everything, and of Christ Jesus, who while testifying before Pontius Pilate made [that same] good confession, I charge you to keep this command without spot or blame until the appearing of the Lord Jesus Christ, which God will bring about in his own time.

The *this* in this passage (flee from all *this*) is referring to the things previously stated in verses 3–10, which mention in part false teachings, controversies, quarrels, envy, strife, malicious talk, evil suspicions, and constant friction between men of corrupt mind. Quite the list! It sounds like the current state of affairs in our land. Let's take a look, break down the word *godliness*, and see just exactly with what Paul is charging Timothy.

The word that is translated as *godliness* comes from a compound Greek word. The first one is *well*, as in well done. The second one is "in worship." Thus, our word means literally "to worship well." It is a direct reference to and extension of the Great Commandment found in Matthew 22:37–40, which says, "Love the Lord your God with all your heart and with all your soul and with all your mind." It is fair to say that anytime one sees this word in the New Testament, it is speaking to worshipping the Lord well. All godliness, be it definitions of, concepts of, or actions of, speaks to and is worship, again aimed at the Lord and King. It must also be understood that ungodliness or godlessness is also worship; it is also worship well. It is just that the focus, the object of that worship, is the antithesis of God, of Jesus. Some would say that that would be the devil. I am not here to argue or belabor that, but I am suggesting that perhaps the antithesis of God is not the devil but self. Ouch. Ultimately, either Jesus or self is on the throne. And there is the rub. I can walk this life with the mindset of "It is not my fault, the devil made me do it" and excuse away my behavior, but someday I am going to stand before my Maker and give account for my life, and that position will not hold up under his standard, his truth. The devil plays a part, no doubt, but I am still responsible for my own thoughts, deeds, and actions. Ouch again.

Paul's writings are most often reactionary; he is responding to something or someone. He is establishing truth, doctrine, and right position in reaction to something that needs correction, or at least adjustment and change. Here, by Paul, Timothy is being challenged and exhorted into godliness. That only means he is or has been struggling to some extent. This is an example of one of the things that makes the Bible so relevant. The Author has no issue with putting our humanity (in this case Timothy's) on display for others to see and understand, from which we can learn and grow. There is no condemnation or judgment here, just honesty and integrity on the part of the One who created it all. Timothy is not alone. We all struggle; we all need help. My heart is fickle sometimes. It fears and manipulates. It is unstable sometimes. It doubts. It is even wicked sometimes (Jeremiah 17:9). It knows, loves, and lives in God's truth, holiness, and righteousness and yet diminishes, ignores, and even kicks against all of that sometimes. My heart needs help—it needs the Savior every day! Timothy did too. You do too, I think. It is always important to remember that sanctification is a lifelong process. It is a journey.

Mix this sobering truth with the intense call to godliness, and you have the basis for these three Beatitudes. Godliness is cousin to mercy, purity, and peacemaking. Living in godliness is closely connected to being merciful, pure, and peaceful. To be godly, to be exercising godliness, is to be like God in the inner man. Walking in godliness is not limited to these three elements, but they do comprise a goodly portion of it.

Bless-ed are the *merciful:* those exercising mercy, those flowing within the heart of God, of Jesus, of the Merciful One. Immersed. Exercising mercy, yes, but more. It is flowing in a state of mercifulness toward others because one has been and is immersed in mercy. Having been affected, one affects. The word reflects compassion, or being compassionate. Compassion is the very thing that drove Jesus. He had compassion on them (Matthew 9:36, 14:14). In some ways, Jesus was a driven man; all of his energies were aimed at the Father, out of which came this overwhelming love and compassion for his creation. It is truly beyond measure. And it is his to live within and give away to others.

In this form, the word merciful occurs only twice in the New Testament. It is found also in Hebrews 2:17, referring to Jesus. It says, "He had to be made like his brothers in every way, in order that he might become a merciful and faithful high priest in service to God." He had to become one of us in order to fully relate to us, in order to fully engage us, in order to fully immerse us into him, into his mercy.

From its usage in both Classical Greek and the New Testament, this word means compassion, mercy, and pity. There is a sense of activity within its expressions. It is to have compassion, to be sorry for, and to show mercy. It is "the emotion roused by contact with an affliction which comes undeservedly on someone else."[1] Yes, this mercy is focused toward others, toward someone else, with the operative words in this definition being *affliction* and *undeservedly*. And, yes, it certainly can be emotional, but that would simply be the outward expression of an inward dynamic. Again, this phenomenon within the heart drove Jesus. It drove him all the way to the Cross. Emotion falls far short of that heart decision and action.

There is an interesting and important undertone found within the depth of this word. Its counterpart in Hebrew offers "a completely different background of thought"[2] than does the Greek word. In the latter, our word has all to do with the actions of the mind and heart. In the former, it is actually a legal term, which gives it even more weight. It means "proper covenant behavior; the solidarity which the partners in the covenant owe one another. This may result in one [covenant partner] giving help to the other in his need."[2] When God established covenant with us through the Cross and all that it entailed, we became covenant partners with him, assuming that we have said yes to Jesus and that we are born again. This legal transaction puts us in the place wherein we receive help from him in our need; he is obligated. As his partner, it also places us in alignment with him in the extension of his merciful ways toward others. Thus, we will receive mercy.

Bless-ed are the *pure* in heart. In the context of some extended worship and intercession, one day I had a vision. It was one scene. I saw running water bubbling, clear, cool, and crisp. Then the vision became apprehensible to me. It was water running from a kitchen faucet pouring over some dishes in the sink. There were some soap bubbles on the dishes. There was sun shining through a window behind the sink. The sun illuminated the water in such a way that it was brilliant, sparkling in presentation. The intense magnitude of that water was striking to me. I knew the Lord was in the vision, and when it ended, I simply waited for him to bring the interpretation. It is this: In the midst of a simple, routine part of life, there was a conspicuous demonstration of purity that came from him. Purity and presence. It was very attractive, and I was distinctly drawn to it. There was a sense of calm, peace, and a real joy associated with the vision, which came from the freedom found in the state of purity.

This is our word. Pure, clean, clear. Unsoiled, unsullied, unalloyed. "Spiritually clean and pure from the pollution and guilt of sin [and iniquity]."[3] It is not on the outside, not an outward experience. This is in and of the heart; bless-ed are the pure in heart. Void of any and all evil. Pure with the sense of one who differentiates between that which is good and that which is excellent, and who lives in the latter. It is clean in a physical sense. It is also clean in the sense of "free, without things that come between."[4] John 15:3 says, "You are already clean because of the word I have spoken to you." Jesus is indicating that his disciples are already pure because of him, because of the authority in the words he has spoken over them. Hebrews 1:3 says, "The Son is the radiance of God's glory and the exact representation of his being, sustaining all things by his powerful word. After he had provided purification for sins, he sat down at the right hand of the Majesty in heaven." The water in the vision is representative of this radiance, and this in the midst of the act of purification. Purity. Second Peter 1:9 says, "He has been cleansed from his past sins." The word *cleansed* is our word, and it is "to be made pure." The soap bubbles in the vision represent this. In Psalm 24:3–4, David speaks to this when he asks a question and then has it answered. "Who may ascend the hill of the Lord? Who may stand in his holy place? He who has clean hands and a pure heart, who does not lift up his soul to an idol or swear by what is false." There it is: pure in heart. Actually, the word for clean in this instance is an offshoot of pure as well and lends itself to supporting our word. It might be rendered as pure and pure for emphasis. Who may stand close to God? The pure and pure.

Our word has a sibling, which is *sincere.* It is a similar word of kindred spirit that corroborates. Paul says, "And this is my prayer: that your love may abound more and more in knowledge and depth of insight, so that you may be able to discern what is best and may be pure and blameless until the day of Christ." The King

James Version says, "That ye may be sincere and without offense till the day of Christ" (Philippians 1:9–10). And then Peter says, "I have written ... to stimulate you to wholesome thinking" (2 Peter 3:1). All three of these English words can be translated as *sincere*. They come from the same compound Greek word, which literally means "judged by sunlight," or by implication "tested as genuine."[5] It is "free from spot or blemish to such a degree as to bear examination in the full splendor of the sun."[6] This brings us right back to the brilliance of the sunlight in the vision. I would suggest an extension and a further definition here would be to bear examination in the full splendor of the *Son*, because it is all about and unto him. Remember these Beatitudes are character traits of Jesus first, and the means to life in him second.

There are two themes running through all of this. One is of relationship—not casual but deep. The other is of his presence, which can't help but be rich and deep. When Jesus is encouraging his disciples, it is in the context of his relationship with them. The writer of Hebrews is talking about the glorious presence of the Son. This is referencing his relationship with his Father while also recognizing his presence alongside his Father. David is asking about being in the presence of God. Paul's charge to be blameless, or without offense, and Peter's mention of wholesome thinking are both aimed at interactions with other people, which is relationship. To be closely examined in the sunlight is not just casually relational, it is intimate. I study my wife in the sunlight and am enthralled with her beauty. There is nothing casual about that!

[Selah]

This is not easy or pleasant, but perhaps in order to even better understand the meaning and value of our word *pure*, we would do well to define *impure*. It carries several meanings within the

New Testament. It can mean unclean or unholy. It also can mean evil or filth. Its most poignant meaning is "a state of moral filthiness, especially in relation to sexual sin; sexual impurity."[7] Webster offers these definitions: "dirty, unclean, defiled, immoral, obscene, unchaste, mixed, adulterated."[8] This is quite the list of ugliness and despair. Perhaps the most direct statement from Scripture regarding impure is found in 1 Thessalonians 4:7, which says, "For God did not call us to be impure, but to live a holy life." There is more weight and significance to that sentence than may be seen at first glance. That is because well into the twenty-first century, as sad and unfortunate as it is, much of what has just been offered by way of defining pure has been discounted, diluted, dismissed, and rejected by much of society. Consciences have no doubt been seared, but depressingly so, it has gone well past that. In the interest of self-gratification and self-satisfaction, hearts have been hardened, and much of what is offered in Romans 1 (especially verses 18–32) has come to pass. I don't say that to judge or even criticize, but to reiterate the truth that even though the world around us has shifted and changed so very much, the Creator, Lord, and King has not. And from there it is simply one's choice as to which master will be served – that of self and what the world has to offer, or the Lord Jesus Christ. I will let God speak for himself: Revelation 21:22–27 says,

> I did not see a temple in the city, because the Lord God Almighty and the Lamb are its temple. The city does not need the sun or the moon to shine on it, for the glory of God gives it light, and the Lamb is its lamp. The nations will walk by its light, and the kings of the earth will bring their splendor into it. On no day will its gates ever be shut, for there will be no night there. The glory and honor of the nations will be brought into it. Nothing impure will ever enter it, nor will anyone

> who does what is shameful or deceitful, but only those whose names are written in the Lamb's book of life.

This is a very strong word. Thank God for his mercy and grace, and his heart to help us.

After Jesus had just had conversation with a man who was trying to manipulate the truth and gain eternal life through his own understandings and works—and discovered that that was not going to work—the man walked away discouraged. The disciples then asked Jesus, "Who then can be saved?" Jesus looked intently at them and said, "With man this is impossible, but with God all things are possible" (Matthew 19:16–26).

[Selah]

Bless-ed are the *pure* in heart. The understanding from Scripture is that the heart is the seat or the center of human life. It is "the core, the base, the place where desires, feelings, affections, passions, thoughts, attitudes and actions stem from."[9] "The causative source of a person's psychological life"[10] says it well. It is that place where the inner man resides. The pure in heart are those whose center of life, whose focus and focal point of life has been made pure by Jesus Christ. Jesus is pure in heart. He has invited—commanded, actually—those who follow him to be the same. Purity is the call.

As I was studying and meditating on this phrase "pure in heart," the Father said to me, "Holiness and righteousness and purity are what I want from you; if you will follow me, they are what I will have with you." This is a very poignant statement and stirred in me several questions. "Just exactly what are you saying, Lord? Just exactly what does that look like? I certainly do not have the innate ability within my heart to live there, to accomplish that.

How do I, how do we do that together?" To which he responded, "Be holy as I am holy." This comes from 1 Peter 1:16. That did not answer my question! A further examination of this and similar passages revealed this: holiness is something established by God being God. He did not attain holiness; he is holy. We gain holiness by aligning our hearts with his. It is a command. It is also a gift freely given. We don't manufacture holiness; we receive it by faith. The more we pursue him, the deeper we go in him, the more his holiness wells up within us. Righteousness is the same. We are righteous; we are the righteousness of Christ by his actions on the Cross (1 Corinthians 1:30). We don't manufacture righteousness; we receive it by faith. The more we pursue him, the deeper we go in him, the more his rightness wells up within us. I am being intentionally redundant to drive a point. His part is to bring his holiness and righteousness to us. Our part is to walk in purity so that we become vessels worthy of his holiness and righteousness. The more we do our part, the more intentional we are in our pursuit of him, which is what enables us to do our part, the more of him we find in us. A pure heart is both the call and the result.

Because purity is my part, the decisions and the choices I make bring me either closer to or farther from purity. This is not performance. I choose to take a shower and wear a nice shirt that she likes on a date night, but that is not me performing for my wife. It is me loving my wife and, in that love, wanting to please her. Taking that further, it is me having studied my wife and discovering that she prefers clean, shaven, and sharp attire to something else. If I had a wife who preferred something different, out of my study of her and love for her, I would adjust to that. Choosing to live, to adjust my thoughts and actions to live in purity, is not performing for God. It is actually the opposite. Performing places the emphasis on the performer, on me. Learning the subtleties, the nuances of relationship (again, by studying the other) and going there places the emphasis on the other. Paraphrased, 2 Timothy 2:15 says, to "Study eagerly so you can stand near the purifying, tempering process, the Temper-er." The more I study him by his Word, through worship and prayer, and by simply hanging out with him, the closer to him I can stand and the more purified I become.

Choosing to be pure, to live in purity, is part of being "transformed through the renewing of my mind" (Romans 12:2). I am not formulaic in my relationship with the Lord. I do, however, recognize more and more that as life goes on, there are certain processes, principles, and criteria that are very productive in contributing to the ongoing betterment of relationships, whether human or divine. Why would I not want to please Jesus? He only saved me from myself and eternal damnation. He only loved me and loves me at the complete sacrifice of himself. He is only in constant pursuit of me. So why would I not want to please him, to pursue and love him back?

Living within the well-defined parameters of life found within Scripture helps me immensely in my decisions and in my choices to walk in purity. Those choices align me with the Lord, which gives access to his help and assistance, so I can become holy and righteous. "Make every effort … to be holy; without holiness no one will see the Lord" (Hebrews 12:14).

The beauty of this is that God never calls us or commands us to something that he is not prepared to help us with. This principle was touched on in chapter 1 and bears repeating here: In Hebrews 11:6, it says that without faith, it is impossible to please God. That's a tall order. But in Ephesians 2:7–8, it says that faith is a gift, with the implication (based on the reference to his incomparable riches of grace and kindness) to take as much as you need. There it is: whenever God establishes an order for life, a command, he offers with it the ways and means to live it out with him. This tenet is found all throughout Scripture and is clear evidence of his grace and mercy at work. Said another way, all that he says and does is rooted in relationship, and he truly is with us in our walk through this life and our pursuit of him. He wants the best for us. More important, he wants the best with us.

And here is why: "for they will see God." Wow! What an amazingly powerful statement. Have you ever actually seen God? Do you know anyone who has? Me neither. Yes, there are those who have testimony of being in the presence of God in such a manner as to have seen his face, but that is quite rare. And yet here it is, written and read in broad daylight: the offer to see God! I have prayed for this for years. I want to see the face of Jesus on this side of glory!

Our word *see* is "to see with the eyes."[11] "As I see the sun setting over the mountains," is an example. It is also "to stare" or "to stare at,"[11] which makes it an intense word. It is not casual by any means because the word has an element of intentionality within it. "I find myself staring at the beauty of my wife in the glow of the warm light," captures the deep, penetrating expression of it. And yet there is more. "To see" is about the physical, but it is equally about perceiving; it is the sensitivity to the awareness of some object or person. There is a dimension of discerning within its meaning; it is "to come to understand as the result of perception."[12] It might be offered as to see with the eye, to perceive with the mind, so as to comprehend with the soul.

It has been said, "Become pure in heart until you see God. Then do what you see him doing." That is combining John 5:19 with our Beatitude. Jesus said in John 5:19, "I can do nothing by myself; I can only do what I see my Father doing" (paraphrase mine). Although our word is different than the one in John, they are synonyms. This statement strongly highlights what is being offered in this Beatitude. It has all to do with pressing in to a deeper life with Jesus. He is speaking clearly, emphatically inviting us to live in this state of purity. This is his heart for us. It is also his command to us, for the sake of depth and intimacy with us. There is nothing more that he wants than this.

Bless-ed are the *peacemakers*. The only time this word is used in the New Testament is here. However, the principle within the characterization of the word is core to the heart of God and is found throughout his Word. Initially, the word refers to "one who works for peace."[13] Clearly found within this word is the understanding of reconciliation: it is "to cause a state of peace or reconciliation between persons."[14] One who is a peacemaker is not one who actually causes peace; that assignment belongs to God. It is one who is closely connected to the Lord and is used to help others come into peace, with one another and/or with situations and circumstances causing unrest and fear.

As this is the only time the word is used, we do well to break it apart and consider the word *peace*. Perhaps the best way to define that word is to look at its Hebraic counterpart, which is *shalom*. The Septuagint uses this word more than 250 times to translate shalom, so it is a good match. Shalom encompasses wholeness, soundness, health, well-being, prosperity, peace as opposed to war, and concord as opposed to strife. As peacemaker has an element of reconciliation within it, so it is with shalom. It has much to do with total and complete reconciliation of self with God; peacemaker brings that reconciliation to others. Shalom comes from God alone and is fully independent of any and all outside conditions. It is a fruit of the Spirit, part of his character. It is "the general sense of well-being, the source and giver of which is Yahweh alone." It includes "everything given by God in all areas of life, in the widest sense of the word."[15] As shalom comes solely from God, it is closely associated with his presence, which is found when there is a living wholeness of consecration to him (see

Matthew 5:48). This supports what we have been talking about all along. Those in shalom are "blessed, guarded, and treated graciously by the Lord."[16]

Returning to our word *peacemaker*, we can now see this principle found within the word. The peacemaker "is not simply one who makes peace between two parties, but one who spreads the good news of the peace [the shalom] of God which he has experienced." Also, "the one who, having received the peace of God in his own heart, brings peace to others."[17] This is a core value from the heart of God to all creation, to his Kingdom. This world we live in is not about us, or just about us; it is more about others. From Matthew 22, to love your neighbor as yourself is to focus on him and not self. This establishes priorities in esteeming others more highly than self (Philippians 2:3). This is what and who Jesus is, who the Father is. Core to them means it needs to be core to us. See it like this: one of the reasons we receive from the Lord blessings and healings and the like, is to let those same things flow through us to others. Freely you have received, freely give (Matthew 10:8). I once knew a leader who insisted that when developing people and building ministry entities, when multiplying things out, one should give the best away. Don't harbor or manipulate to hang on to those you think are the best—give them away and release them into the next thing their Lord has for them. This principle works because it matches the generosity, the heart, of God.

Those flowing in the realm of peacemaker are called sons of God. This can also be translated as daughters of God. This is because they are in a place wherein they are imitating and shadowing the heart of the Son. They are taking on the character of Jesus, their friend and brother (Proverbs 18:24; John 15:13–15), in ushering in the shalom of God and in ministering it to others. They are allowing Jesus to flow through them; they are like the Son, so they are sons. If you are a son of God, because he is the Son of

God, you are brother to him. If you are a son of God, you are one whom Father God loves and cherishes as only the Father can. This brings shalom.

Bless-ed are those exercising the mercy of God toward others, the spiritually clean and pure in heart, and the deliverers of shalom to all around them, for they will be shown mercy, they will see God, and they will be called sons of God and walk as brothers to the Christ.

Mercy, purity, shalom. These are deep elements of God's heart. They are central, fundamental, and foundational to the very essence of who he is. Yet today they are regularly ignored, underplayed, belittled, and even mocked by much of society. We live in a world that is often ugly, and seems to be getting uglier. Wrong is the new right. Foolishness is the new wisdom. Lawlessness is rapidly becoming the new law. The elements of the impurity referenced above are exalted. Peace is something many try to buy in order to pacify the guilt and the shame that comes from being wrong and impure. Jesus said, "In this world you will have trouble" (John 16:33b). That was quite the understatement. The rest of that same verse says, "But take heart! I have overcome the world" (John 16:33c). As dark as things may seem or may become, there is One on the throne who will not be denied. He will continue to be the heart and source of mercy, purity, and the peace that goes beyond understanding (Philippians 4:7). And he will continue to look for and align with those who say, "Here am I. Send me." in response to the question, "Whom shall I send? And who will go for us?" (Isaiah 6:8).

I stated in the beginning of this book, "What the Beatitudes bring to the table is revolutionary to the twenty-first century. They offer a means of living life that is totally contrary to the collective understanding, the common knowledge of the day … They are totally amazing and, if embraced and followed, bring not only a new perspective but a new manner of life." He will have a people who bow down and worship him, and from that place of being fully yielded to his Lordship, they'll follow his every move. The Beatitudes offer that. They bring that. I cannot even begin to express the intensity, the passion, the insistence within which these words are coming as I write them. There is such an amazing, overwhelming passion and compassion you, Lord, are sharing that you have for your creation. You would that none would perish, but that all would come to you and spend eternity with you (2 Peter 3:9). You want all to be in a deep, rich, wonderful, and delightfully intimate relationship with you. Forever. In that, you are seeking those who are seeking you that they might become sweet, humble vessels through which you can pour yourself out so others may enter in and do and be the same. These words, these definitions, and these truths we are studying all speak to others; they are all aimed at the other people with whom we share the planet. You are giving of yourself through us giving of ourselves, for your glory and the gain of others. Amazing.

Help us, Lord, to see, to sense, to feel, and to capture your heart here. Help us to say yes to you in all the fullness you want and intend for and with us. There are no stronger words. The development of the inner man for your glory, for your work on earth, is plainly seen and completely established early in these Beatitudes. The work of your heart, coming through that now fully-developed inner man, is what you want. It is the work of mercy, the work of purity, the work shalom you seek. Especially now. Help us, Lord. We want you. We need you. We want you to have your will, your way. Come, Lord Jesus. "And the Spirit and the bride say come" (Revelation 22:17).

Chapter 10

Points of Application

What is the overall practical application of these Beatitudes, of this most important communication from Jesus? Certainly it is not just to know and understand.

Many years ago, I was an outside sales rep for a major company. It was a rewarding career path; it was also complex and sometimes difficult work. It was common to meet for morning coffee with the others in the sales crew to talk shop. Every time we gathered, one gentleman would have two cups of coffee, black. After a time of discussion and comparing notes together, and well into his second cup, he would pick up his cup, announce, "Well, I guess I'd better go do something," take the last sip, smack the cup down on the table, and add, "Even if it's wrong." He was salesman of the year most every year. I spent the first thirty-plus years of my life in Minnesota, the "land of ten thousand lakes." Think fish. A very common statement in those parts regarding an action needing to take place was "Either fish or cut bait." In other words, either get to fishing or get to preparing to get to fishing, but don't just sit around and do nothing. In the movie *Shawshank Redemption*, at one point in the story, the main character, Andy Dufresne, says, "It's time to either get busy living, or get busy dying." When personalized, these statements can create a tension within. This is because the natural man tends to the status quo; we tend to resist change, so we stay put. We may get determined to change, and we read and research for a while, gaining knowledge. Then we do nothing about it. Over time, the net result is that we know more but act less. To cut to the quick, yet another way of saying this is that we humans tend toward laziness and complacency. Ouch. And we live in a society that is overrun with these phenomena.

On the other hand, there is the option to apply what has been learned. When I was ten or eleven, I got my first opportunity to drive the family boat. We had a cabin on a large lake, and my dad had taken the family on an afternoon cruise across the bay. When we reached the other side, my dad asked me if I knew where home was. "Yes, it is right next to that tree," I responded as I pointed back across the bay to a very large elm tree that stood head and shoulders above the pine trees surrounding it. "Take us home," he said. I was ecstatic to say the least, as you might imagine. The little boy gets his first shot at being "the man" in control of this monstrous, noble steed. Okay, I admit it was just a simple, humble little boat—but not to my eyes! My chest pounding, my heart in my throat, away we went.

After a very short time, my sisters started complaining that they were getting sick from my driving. The interchange that followed was nothing short of amazing. Dad said, "Where are you going?" "I'm headed toward that tree." "Where are your eyes?" "On the bow of the boat. I am lining up the bow with the tree." "Look behind you." What I saw was revelatory. The motor of the boat leaves a trail of bubbles. That trail looked like a snake trying hard to slither away—it was anything but straight! Then he said it: "Keep your eyes on the tree." That statement rings true in my soul even today. As I adjusted my sight, I gained a significantly different perspective and found myself relaxing into the journey. A few minutes later he said, "Now look back." What was now behind me was a smooth, straight line. I had been trying to align the nose of the boat with the height of the tree. My focus was very narrow, very short. I had been seriously overcompensating—thus the pattern of the wake I was leaving behind me, and thus my sisters' complaints. When I applied what I had just learned, the results were incredible. And from that experience came a broader application that is profound and still with me today: Where are your eyes? Keep your eyes on the tree. Wow.

In this life, Jesus is that tree. When my eyes are on him, it is well with my soul, and I can relax into him. It is then that the perceptions, the outlook, the line of life is significantly straighter and easier than when my eyes are on me and my circumstances. When my focus is on me, my sight is short, which finds me continually overcompensating, overreacting. When my focus is on the Lord and King, life takes on a much higher purpose and value, which yields an inner stability, a peace. From that place, I am much more encouraged and motivated.

One of the most applicable Scriptures in my life is Philippians 4:4–9. In verse 9, Paul draws it together by simply but powerfully saying, "Put it to practice." There it is: the directive we all need over and over again. Bring all things learned beyond the gathering of knowledge and into the flow of life, into the daily grind. Put it all into practice. How does this apply itself to you and me today? In the overall course of the Beatitudes, we are now turning a corner. The first four established the life of Jesus within the soul and then aligned that with the heart of Jesus. The next three gave breadth and depth to that base as seen, expressed, and exercised through mercy, purity, and peace. These seven elements, having been melded together into a strong, solid, and viable entity, now continue the journey into tangible living, into an applicable reality. This is clearly where the rubber meets the road, where we move past concept and full on into the actuality of living life fully by way of these Beatitudes. I have chosen four areas of application that lend themselves directly from the context within which we have been immersed, both spiritually and tangibly. They are as follows.

1) Developing the innate ability to hear the voice of God

2) Coming to shalom in the depth of the inner-man

3) Practically and authentically dealing with issues of justice and injustice

4) Managing the sober reality of spiritual warfare

Each of these could be a book of their own. In this context, I will address each head-on, bringing the dinkum oil to the table. Dinkum oil is an Australian slang phrase that means "the honest, genuine truth."

Recently, I worked with a couple for some time, mentoring them as they worked at developing a deeper walk with Jesus. She had had a significant encounter with the Lord in the night, which drew her to a renewed hunger for more. Together they wanted to get more serious and press in to a deeper, more meaningful relationship with Jesus. Over time, she began to have dreams almost weekly. For a few months, she had different dreams that all had the same interpretation, which was of great significance. The sense was that the Lord was saying, "You're not ready. Get ready."

Over and over, week after week, she heard the message: "You're not ready. Get ready." It didn't take too long to realize that what the Lord was communicating, although clearly for them in the context of their deepening walk with him, was also for the whole of the populace who call on the name of Jesus.

Holy Spirit was—and is—saying it is imperative that we get ready certainly for the day in which we live, but even more so for the times that are approaching. We need to be prepared and equipped for that which is coming, for that which has already started to come our way. I am not here to discuss the political or social dynamics of this present danger in our neighborhoods, cities, or nation. I am here to illuminate the urgency of the need to get ready. Have you ever noticed that Holy Spirit is the same Holy Spirit everywhere you go? He may bring his message through the context of the local area, but the heart of the message is the same. It might be conveyed through water in Minnesota, corn in Iowa, concrete in New York or Los Angeles, or mountains in Colorado, but his heart (and what proceeds from it) is the same for all people everywhere. I say that to say this: No matter which ministry, network, or group one listens to or is connected to, there is the message of an urgency in the air in the day in which we are living. That is God calling, alerting, warning, and drawing his people.

My wife and I raised four children who are now all adults and live in four different regions of the country. It is not very often that we all are together under one roof! That happened just a couple of years ago in our living room for Christmas, and it was delightful. Our tradition has always included a time around the tree where we share the joy of gift giving and receiving one person at a time, so all can focus on the one. We start that time with a prayerful devotional, which usually falls on me. That year I was prompted by the Lord to share in a reflective manner and talk about this: "In light of the Christ, in light of his purposes and intentions surrounding his birth, death, and resurrection, it needs to be seen that it is no mistake that we, the whole of us, including spouses and grandchildren, have been placed together in one family, in this family. We could have been born or placed into different families, at different times, and in different countries. It is no coincidence that each was born or married into this family, was placed into this country, at this time in history. It is by design, sovereign and divine, that we are family. There is a calling on each of us, individually and collectively, that can be fulfilled in no other manner or time frame than the one we are in." I shared about this dream interpretation to bring home this point: it is no longer an option for any of us to take or live life in a casual manner. We must position and prepare ourselves, individually and as a family, for where we are to be and where we are headed.

This message is not just for my family. To be intentionally redundant, it is for all who call on the name of Jesus; it is imperative, and there is an urgency in it.

To get ready—or perhaps to extend this to its natural conclusion, to be ready—is to come to that place wherein we live day by day, even moment by moment, in his presence. We live well past the concepts and fully into the practices and intimacies of righteousness, holiness, and purity—all from him, all with him. As has been previously stated, this then becomes our life and lifestyle.

The heart of this communiqué from the Lord, to get and stay ready, is this: it is to come into the place of depth and intimacy with Jesus wherein we are willing and able to hear and respond to his voice clearly, readily, and without hesitation, doubt, or uncertainty.

1. Developing the innate ability to hear the voice of God

To *hear*. The word has a double meaning. It is the perception of sound, of tone. It is also to hear, respond, and obey. This word embraces both hearing with the ear and capturing something with the mind. It is not trivial; it is not simply hearing a bird and understanding it is a bird. It is actually "the apprehension and acceptance by the mind of the content of what was heard."[1] There is a sense of grasping hold of, or seizing, with the mind what has been heard by the ear. The root word in Greek is *akouo*. One of its forms is *hypakouo*, which translates to "hear beneath," and that is to obey.[2] This is attentive listening directly connected to a response of obedience. It demands attention, acceptance, and engagement. It assumes these three words and the principles they represent.

To expand this a bit further, Jesus said in John 10:27, "My sheep hear my voice, and I know them, and they follow me" (NASB). This verse sheds light on our word. The word *voice* is literally *tone*, or "a tone." One of the definitions of *hear* is the perception of tone. A mother knows the cry of her own baby in a crowd of crying babies; she knows her baby's tone. "My people hear my tone …" I want to know your tone, Jesus. I want to seek your tone. There are so many tones out there. I want to hear and be attuned to your tone. I want to know the quality, the frequency, the pitch, and the resonance of your tone, Jesus. The verse might read, "My sheep hear, understand, respond to, obey the disclosure, the revelation of my tone, which is a manifestation of my heart" (paraphrase mine).

To be ready is to hear him and respond accordingly. The more we hear, the more we respond, and the more righteous, holy, and pure we become. There is a knowing here that is well past the physical realm and well into the spiritual one. Getting and being ready is just that. When we are trained by him into this hearing and responding to him, we are equipped for whatever may come, good, bad, or otherwise. When we are yielded to him so as to be submitted into that training process, we are where he wants and needs us to be. There he can fully protect and guide us according to his way and will. This is the only way to depth, to the familiarity, closeness, and intimacy the Lord wants for and with us.

> The voice, [the tone], of the Spirit is as gentle as a zephyr [a gentle, mild breeze], so gentle that unless you are living in perfect communion with God, you never hear it. The checks of the Spirit come in the most extraordinarily gentle ways, and if you are not sensitive enough to detect his voice, [his tone], you will quench it, and your personal spiritual life will be impaired. His checks [and his encouragements and directives] always come as a still small voice.[3]

This training process is perhaps best illustrated from a military perspective. Not militaristic—that is not it. But in this manner: The soldier goes through a process of training and equipping, over and over again, until he has it perfected and it becomes automatic; in this context, it would then become a lifestyle. Then he is set and ready for whatever comes his way well before the event, well before any actual engagement for which he has been trained. He has been trained, then, to live in a state of preparedness, which includes a state of anticipation, of expectation. For example, I have a friend who has a job, an assignment, as a bodyguard for a well-known international speaker. As he engages in this assignment he is always in a stance of readiness. There are a number of things he must do mentally and physically to be in this place. One such thing is that his body weight is always on the balls of his feet, never on the heels. This is not obvious to the casual observer and may seem like a trivial thing, yet it is anything but. This position makes him ready. It gives him the upper hand, the upper edge at every moment, not just physically but mentally. That stance makes him alert. It makes him ready. That is the call for us. It's not necessarily in a position of defense, or warfare, although that may be a part. It is much more in a wonderful position of intimacy, of presence, of simply being in and with Jesus, with Father, and with Holy Spirit.

There is a pattern to be seen here that is vital in our lives with and in Christ, no matter the day in which we live. I touched on this earlier in chapter 4, and it is called sanctification. The more we yield to him and his work within us, the healthier and more healed we become. As that is transpiring, we are then drawn deeper and become more intimate with him. From that place, we more easily hear and more willingly respond, and on and on into eternity. This pattern is essential to embrace and live out. This is how we go to the deep places in him and stay there. Remember, it is this for which we have been created.

When it comes to hearing, we must understand that the Lord is not lacking for words. He spoke all that we know into existence. He was speaking before the Word was written, and he has been speaking ever since. The Word is the standard from which we must measure all things, which includes all dialogue. That having been acknowledged, he is continually communicating and engaging us. One of the biggest challenges for us humanoids is that we don't listen very well, and consequently we can't hear very well. To come into complete understanding, and then into the fullness of life as it is offered in these Beatitudes, requires that we hear and respond, that we learn from the Master, the Tamer, how to hear and respond.

This principle may be best captured within the definition and concept of the Hebrew word *shema*.[4] In the form considered here, the word comes into English as "to hear." In our language and way of life, *listen* and *hear,* although not the same, are similar. That's not so in Hebraic culture. In our Western lifestyle, we tend to weigh and ponder. We may give consideration to what we are listening to, what we hear; we may draw some conclusion, and then we may or may not make a response. In the Eastern Hebraic worldview, it is not like that. For them, to listen was to hear, and to hear was to respond. They had no comprehension otherwise; they could not do otherwise. It was undivided attention so as to understand how to respond. It was to hear with attention and obedience. Clearly, in the definition of shema, is seen the action of hearing—not the action of the ear physically hearing a voice, but the response of action to the words heard. This was their way of life. In our culture, we might best understand this as "to heed," which is "to give careful attention to," with the assumption of reaction. When my children were young, one of the things they heard from me over and over again was, "Listen and obey, and do it right away!" That portrays it. What I was conveying to them was the principle of an immediate, positive, obedient response to what they were hearing. So it is with *shema*.

As Hebrew is a pictorial language, our word *shema* paints a very intriguing scene. The word can also translate as "to see the name." Interesting. The word *name* literally translates to "what destroys chaos." Very interesting! So our word can be "to see what destroys chaos."[5] We could say it as "to see what creates order." And here is where it becomes quite remarkable and revelatory. *Hear, understand,* and *obey* are all spelled exactly the same—they are all the same word![5] This is one of the reasons Hebrew is such a difficult language to understand and translate. In this case, the same spelling can have one of three different English meanings depending on where the word is located in the context of the phrase, the sentence, or the immediate surroundings of that sentence. Thus, "to hear" is "to destroy chaos"; "to understand" is "to destroy chaos"; "to obey" is "to destroy chaos." Wow! Each word speaks clearly to order, to that which brings order. Generally, when we "listen and obey, and do it right away," we are entering into and aligning with the one who brought the communication we are hearing. When that someone is God, the Creator of it all, the Almighty One who is deeply in love with us and in pursuit of us, that brings great order. That changes things!

There is yet one more insight to glean from this: the sense of anticipation. As my friend is constantly in that state in his assignment as a bodyguard, so it must be with us in our relationship with the Lord. I listened to an interview years back with Wayne Gretzky, one of the most prolific hockey players to ever play the game. The part of the interview I remember was when he was asked the question, "What makes you so great?" His response was quite enlightening and hits the mark here. He said, "If that is true, then it would be because most players in this game go to where the puck is. I go to where it is going." There it is. He had the innate ability to anticipate where the flow of the game was going and be there when it happened. This is what being ready is all about: anticipating, hearing, and responding. The Lord wants to develop that innate ability within us not just individually but corporately. How exciting is that?

Bringing all this back to the interpretation of these dreams and its directive to listen, to be in that place where we are always listening, always hearing, and then always yielding and responding in obedience without question, makes us ready. I believe that is the order, the application of the day.

I would be remiss if I did not include the following. If you are not hearing his voice, (a) it may be that you are not one of his sheep. If that is so, today is the day to change that. Seek him, talk to him, and ask him in; he is faithful and will respond. Feel free to contact us through our website for any questions you may have or any help you may need. Or, (b) it may be you are not in position to hear; you are not positioned, you have not positioned yourself, or you have not purposed to position yourself. He is continually speaking. Your job is to position yourself to receive, to hear what he is saying. What does that look like? It looks like getting past your self, your way, your agenda. It looks like submission, like yielding to him and his agenda. It looks like these Beatitudes. It is committing to a lifestyle that embraces more and more of him and his ways, and less and less of you and your ways. It means getting serious, perhaps for the first time, about the spiritual disciplines of time, energy, and effort toward God. It is to purpose to read and study, to pray and intercede, to worship and fast. It is sacrificial living in his direction. "But seek first his Kingdom and his righteousness; and all these things shall be added to you" (Matthew 6:33 NASB). Learn to, purpose to, seek him first and most of all, and all else will come together. Focus and pay attention to the things that are important to him, and he will focus and pay attention to the things that are important to you.

2. Coming to shalom in the depth of the inner man

At the end of the day, how I deal with justice and injustice in my world, and how I manage me in the midst of any conflict or point of tension, has to do with my level of confidence in the Lord. At the end of the day, the manner in which I embrace, take in, and apply the Beatitudes to my heart and to my life has all to do with my level of confidence in me in him. They are directly and intentionally connected. As this section unfolds, you will see this clearly.

We have talked at length about shalom. The question here is just how one goes about living there. The inner man is where all things live, good, bad, and ugly. My thought life, my actions and attitudes, what comes from my mouth, my body language, my love expressed and received, and my strongholds all spring from there.

A stronghold is accurately defined as a "house of thoughts." It has nothing inherently to do with God or the devil; it simply amounts to my collection of thoughts and resultant conclusions. Other words for this are "worldview" or "perspective." The devil works to develop strongholds in my mind. So does God. Part of "being transformed through the renewing of [my] mind" (Romans 12:2b) is allowing God to change, to transform my strongholds.

I had a vision one day while hanging out with my wife. We were talking and sharing life, and all of a sudden the Lord came to me with a vision. Try paying attention, supposedly undivided attention, to your spouse while the Lord downloads a vision. His grace was sufficient in the moment, is all I can say! In the vision, I was standing in a particular place, on a smooth, flat surface. As it unfolded, I saw walls develop around me. They were smooth and took on a cylindrical form, perhaps like the inside of a silo. There was no ceiling because it was open as far up as I could see. It was comfortable enough, and I did not feel confined or restricted. As I was standing there and taking in what was before me, I started to see things on the floor and walls. The longer I looked, the uglier my surroundings became. What I was seeing was beyond what I can describe here. It caused me to abhor, to cry; it was revolting. It makes me cry even now as I write.

After a while, Jesus suddenly appeared on my left. We were side by side. I could actually feel a subtle pressure on my shoulder that was outside the vision. As I recognized his presence, I asked him, "What is this? Where are we?" His response was overwhelming to me. "This is the bottom of your soul, Jay. I am showing you this not to judge or condemn, but simply to let you know I am here with you. We are here together, and have been, and will be. All because you asked me in." The vision was over, and my heart was rent. I saw the ugliness of my soul. I saw the pronounced beauty of Jesus. He revealed my pain, my wound, my sin, my sin nature, my propensity to sin, the iniquities, the things done to me and against me, and my reactions. He showed me his care, his compassion, his love, and his unadulterated willingness to walk and live with me—without an ounce of negativity in any manner or expression. By showing me my soul, he showed me his.

[Selah]

He died for all that. He lives for all that. He sent his Spirit to teach, guide, and direct me through all that. He is here to cleanse and heal, to purge and purify, to make me like him. That is his work, and it all happens in the inner man. When I align with him in helplessness and am tamed, in mourning, hungering, and thirsting, I come into his fold and am transformed through the renewing of my mind. The more I submit to him in the process, the more transformed I become. But the more I don't, the more I won't. It is important to recognize the choice here. I can live in my woundedness, or I can live in Jesus. What is essential to see is that there is pain either way. The former perpetrates pain; the latter resolves it.

The inner man is full of all manner of beauty, but also ugliness from sin and being sinned against, and all the multiple sequences and subsequences that follow. This is why we need Jesus. This is why he came and died and rose again. The purpose of the Beatitudes is to help us see, in light of him, just who and what we are within—and then as this is all exposed, to be healed and aligned with him. Again, by showing me my soul, he showed me his and continued to invite me in. The more I ask him to help me and make me wholehearted, the deeper he goes to cleanse me and heal me. His objective is crystal clear. This is his desire for all of us. He would that none would perish, that all would spend eternity with him (2 Peter 3:9). He is coming back for a bride without spot or wrinkle (Ephesians 5:27 KJV), for a bride who looks like and is as he is in heart and character. The inner man is where this all takes place.

There is bitterness in there. It is the spite, the stiff-necked reaction, the stubbornness that comes from life's situations. These are rooted in unforgiveness and rebellion, both of which come from pride. There is fear in there. It is the insecurity, the uncertainty, the hesitancy that comes from the rejections and abandonments, the loneliness. When these things go on repeatedly for years, seemingly forever, they become the seed and breeding ground for hope deferred, and a bitter root can develop (Hebrews 12:15). He is found there, in your soul and mine. The bitter, angry, wounded me can blame God for all my pain, for causing all my pain. This is not true, but it sure does feel that way. The truth is that he came and died and rose again for just exactly that. All he is asking me to do is cooperate with him in his work in my soul. Can I die to my own stuff? Can I release me to him and thus allow him that work? We talked about Job and James; can I allow him that work in me? He wants me and you to accept his work in us. He is asking us to deal with our own hearts in an appropriate manner. Recognize the weakness. Don't be afraid, proud, or rebellious. Release your soul to his. See that Jesus is found in your weakness, in your failures and shortcomings. And see that he is not discounting you by illuminating your inherent, human frailties and inabilities. What he is actually doing is highlighting his strengths and presence in your midst, for your gain and his glory. The vision was not about me. It was all about him in me. The more we see, acknowledge, and embrace this, the more we live in shalom. The Father said to me, "Intimacy, son. It is what you are created for." Bring us all to that truth and reality, Lord.

Jesus walked into my office one evening. He had come two evenings before. I thought it was a high-ranking angel. I was in a deep funk and blew him off. Then two nights later, there stood Jesus. My first reaction was to repent and express my sorrow over being such a selfish jerk. He stood in the doorway and said nothing. A few moments later, he walked to the opposite corner of my desk and again said nothing. After a bit, he moved over to the window and then was gone. He never said a word. But his countenance and silence spoke volumes. He was in a posture of seriousness; he was serious, perhaps stoic, in demeanor. It was to make a point. It was to get me there, to seriousness. He was saying that I was not taking into account the value, the importance of me and who I am. I was not taking myself seriously enough. I also think he was calling me out. He was calling me to account, to realize and embrace once and for all who I am and whose I am in him. It was like he was saying, "Enough wallowing. Enough of slipping back into the pity bag, the pride exercised to protect your wound. It is time to grow past that. Enter into my rest, my shalom." So be it.

The statement made at the beginning of this section now comes to light. One of the primary results of his work in my soul is the healing of my heart. One of the primary results of that healing is confidence. It is not self-confidence but rather a realization of our place and purpose in his heart. When finally we have come to that place of a death to self, and finally we have come to that place of life in him, there is a confidence that rises up. It is not pride or arrogance; it actually has nothing to do with self and its abilities. It is a confidence the Lord has in us. It is his confidence embedded in our souls. The vision of my soul was not about me, and the visitation to my office was not about me. This confidence built up within me is also not about me. It has all to do with his love for me, his delight in me, his assuredness and certainty over me. I am his, and he knows it. He is mine, and I know it. This intimacy is the best place on the planet. It is this that brings shalom to the depth of the inner man. Let's let him take us there.

3. Practically and authentically dealing with issues of justice and injustice

It is important to see that there is justice in the heart of God. Jesus is justice. He came to earth to mete justice. He hung on the Cross to defeat injustice. "He was raised for our justification [which includes our justice]" (Romans 4:25). Within the truth of justification there is the sense of being justified. Said another way, there is justice in being justified.

Because Jesus is justice, once again let's look at him and how he lived his life; he is our example. In Mark 3:5–6, in the context of the Pharisees looking for an excuse to accuse him while he was healing a man on the Sabbath, it says, "He looked around at them in anger and, deeply distressed at their stubborn hearts, said to the man, 'Stretch out your hand.' He stretched it out, and his hand was completely restored. Then the Pharisees went out and began to plot with the Herodians how they might kill Jesus." I said in chapter 7, "The action of justice finds is roots in prautes." This is where that statement fits. Jesus is angry.

(A sidebar here: some would use this Scripture, among others, out of context to support their argument that Jesus is not deity based on his "human" reaction in this situation. They totally miss the point, the thrust of the dialogue. As we will see, this situation does nothing but strongly prove his deity.)

The word *anger* in this context means "wrath; anger as a state of mind." It comes from a word that means "to desire eagerly." It is "to desire with grief."[6] To desire what? It is "a desire to punish the one who has brought hurt, who has hurt in a manner he ought not."[7] Jesus is not just angry. He is angry enough to want to hurt someone! These people are stubborn, hard of heart, and resistant to Jesus, to the Father, and to the Father's pursuits, heart, and plans. They are misleading the entire nation in their attitudes and actions. Jesus is angry with them because they are hurting his Father's heart. Father sent his Son to save them and all those around them. He literally put his heart out there by that action. They have totally missed it and are working hard to help everyone else miss it as well. However, it is vital to see there is no judgment here. There are no conclusions here. Jesus is not the dysfunctional victim acting out here. He is angry. Angry like "If you mess with my wife, you will be sorry," or like a sibling protecting another sibling. And for good reason: these people have fully rejected him and in so doing have hurt his Father. He is not judging or condemning, or casting them off or away. Nor is he lashing out and actually physically hurting someone. Anger here is an expression of his heart, not an action of his flesh. In the same context, in Mark 3:29, after these same people have accused him of casting out demons by the power of the devil, whereas the truth is he did that by the power of the Spirit of God, he reacted in a similar manner. They have compared Holy Spirit with the devil.

On one hand, the depth of love and the connection in the Trinity, the Triune Godhead, is amazing. On the other hand, here is a prime example of justice being meted through the heart and action of prautes. See how Jesus dealt with the intense anger brought on by the intense injustice. What did he do with all that anger, albeit a righteous anger? Mark 3:7 says he "withdrew with his disciples to the lake." He took his friends with him and removed himself from the situation for a time. Luke 6:6–12 tells the same story. Verse 12 has him going "out to a mountainside to *pray*, and spending the night *praying* to God." Matthew 12:9–21 also shares the same story where it says "he withdrew," and then it quotes Isaiah 42:1–4, which says,

> Here is my servant, whom I have chosen, the one I love, in whom I delight; I will put my Spirit on him and he will proclaim justice to the nations. He will not quarrel or cry out; no one will hear his voice in the streets. A bruised reed he will not break, and a smoldering wick he will not snuff out, till he leads justice to victory. In his name the nations will put their hope.

We do well to catch the word *quarrel* and what it brings to the table. It means "to wrangle, to contend." A close synonym is "to fight, to struggle against."[8] To wrangle is "to argue or dispute, especially in an angry manner."[9] Isaiah says he will not do this.

Yes, Jesus was angry, and for good reason, at the injustice of the actions taking place. But see here the main point of the whole story: his response is not to lash out, and it is not to act out in the sense of passive-aggressive behavior, either walking away or getting hostile. Rather, his response is to double down. He is taking that anger and exercising it to pursue all the more, to press into the Father and the resolution of the issue, to "run to the roar," if you will. (More on this at the end of the chapter.) This proactive pursuit is seen in the Father in that he sent his Son in the first place. This is seen in the Son in that he came right back at it. He continued in his assignment, put himself aside, and simply kept with what he had stated in John 5:19, "I only do what I see my Father doing, because whatever the Father does the Son also does" (paraphrase mine). In other words, his anger never became about him. He stayed focused on the One he was serving. He righted wrong, and he brought justice to bear when he hung on that Cross. Through it all, he kept himself in check and was obedient to Father, even unto death (Philippians 2:8). It was prautes in action fighting for justice, fighting against injustice. It is still so today.

The question is, what drives justice? What drives the Lord in bringing, in meting, justice? The answer to that question tells us just how we are to deal with the same. Initially and on one hand, it is compassion. On the other hand, it is acting and living in righteousness and truth, with their setting and settling nature. God is righteousness and truth. He will have justice. When we settle into that, and thus into him, we will see him do what he does. Justice will prevail. When a man lied, cheated, and maneuvered his way into stealing $2,500 from me in a business deal, I asked the Father what he wanted me to do about it. His response says it all: "Nothing. I will bring justice to this situation in my time, in my manner. Yours is to lean into me, pray for him, and trust." I gave a sigh. "Yes, sir. That is exactly what I will do." And I did. By the way, shalom was all over me—not because of me, but because of him in my yieldedness to him.

There is a qualifier here that must be noted. Justice, a correction to justice, and even judgment in the midst of correcting to justice are not negatives. On the contrary, they are a beautiful reality and expression of God's love, passion, and compassion for and on his creation, his people. Justice meted out brings blessing. When the truth comes out and all is settled, there is a resolve and a peace that comes for all parties concerned. How many times have you heard, in the midst of wrong coming to right, "I am so glad the truth is finally out"? What is that? Justice includes revelation, which in its core reveals the truth. And the truth is what sets us free (John 8:32) and so is that which brings peace.

4. Managing the sober reality of spiritual warfare

The practical, realistic, tangible expression and lifestyle of prautes is a powerful manner in which to manage spiritual warfare, primarily on a personal level, but not just. Spiritual warfare is fighting the adversary, the accuser of the brethren (1 Peter 5:8; Revelation 12:10). When we remove his points of confrontation, and when we remove his ability to leverage himself into our lives, we win that battle. When we continue to win battles, we win the war. If not, then we lose. There are a number of forms of effective warfare against the powers of darkness. Dealing with powers and principalities is a discussion for another time and place. Dealing with what is sometimes referred to as ground-level warfare—the enemy coming at you and yours personally, comes into the picture here. Certainly there are times when it is necessary and appropriate to stand strong in the authority given to the believer who is following the Lord Jesus Christ, address the devil, and send him away (Ephesians 6:10–12; James 4:7–8). It is also critical to understand that lifestyle itself, the attitudes carried, the actions taken, and the choices made moment by moment all play a large role in warfare successes and failures. For example, it is true that worship is warfare. When I engage in worship to and of the Lord and King, I am actually engaging him and, by default, disengaging anything the enemy might be throwing at me. If I broaden that to include prayer and intercession, and I bring that to the place encouraged by Paul, "Pray without ceasing," there is little room for the devil to work (Colossians 4:2; 1 Thessalonians 5:17). Obedience to the things of God is also warfare. As I study the Scriptures and apply them to my life, and as I yield to the Word of God and the voice of the Lord, I am exercising obedience to him. There the devil has no play. All of this fully includes what we have been discussing in this book. Right living is warfare. Righteousness is warfare. Holiness and purity are the same. Humility, true humility, is too. All are effective warfare.

One of the most valuable and effective forms of warfare, and intimately entangled within what has just been discussed, is living within the elements of prautes. When we bring prautes to John 14:30b, the enemy has nothing on us. "The prince of this world [the devil] is coming. He has no hold on me." The devil had no hold, he had no leverage, he had nothing on Jesus because of his love for and obedience to his Father, because he was praus. The very same truth applies to us.

Mix this all together and walk it out, and we win! To whom does the earth belong? Who has hold of it? That would be God. Jesus took it back on the Cross. The praus will what? The praus will inherit the earth. That is powerful spiritual warfare.

Note: Running toward the roar

Once, the Lord said to me, "Consider the lion." So I did. I studied them for a season and found them to be fascinating animals. One of the things that was striking to me was the manner in which they hunt. Their methodology is unique and intriguing. They live and hunt in groups, which are called prides; they are family. Their favorite lunch is gazelle. When it comes to hunting, it is the adult females and young adult males that do most of the work. Imagine the scene with me. The wind is blowing north to south. On the south side of a green, grassy field full of grazing gazelle, the group responsible for the kill place themselves roughly in a semicircle, hiding in the brush downwind from their prey. On the north side of the field sits Old Man Lion, perhaps noticed and perhaps not; either way, there's no immediate threat. He's still the head of the pride, but he can't run fast, and he has lost most of his teeth. He is not really much for battle anymore, but he can roar like nobody's business. When everyone is in place and the time is right, he goes to work, roars, and scares the daylights out of the gazelle.

The Lord said, "Consider the gazelle; consider their conflict." So I did. I pondered: They are now quite afraid of what to them is their archenemy and a sure means of death. Having now heard the lion, he is also in their sight; their source of conflict is fully identified. Instinctively, they take off running as fast as they can. They head away from that scary and horrible roar and end up where? Right into the path, right into the jaws, of the rest of their archnemeses. End of story.

Holy Spirit used this story to teach me a principle for life when he said to me, "Run toward the roar; learn to run toward the roar." If the gazelle knew to run toward Old Man Lion, they would flee unharmed. That action would probably scare him as much as them, and he would start running away from them! Even if he chased them, they would be able to outrun him and resolve their conflict. This principle, this approach, can be applied to many of life's circumstances. Think about it. If we face the conflict, the source of trouble, the cause of the aggravation; if we advance toward it instead of running from it, it becomes a workable, manageable, and even surmountable issue. This finds application in the realm of spiritual warfare. Perhaps of more import, this also finds application in all manner of relationships, in inner man issues, in work and social arenas, and more. Run from evil; resist the enemy, yes (James 4:7). But choose to run toward the roar, toward the points of tension and conflict in life. Face the fear head-on. When done with prayer and within prautes, this is a powerful tactic in the resolution of life's troubles.

Chapter 11

The Day in Which We Live

Matthew 5:10–12 says, "Bless-ed are those who are persecuted because of righteous, for theirs is the Kingdom of heaven. Bless-ed are you when people insult you, persecute you and falsely say all kinds of evil against you because of me … [on account of me]. Rejoice and be glad, because great is your reward in heaven, for in the same way they persecuted the prophets who were before you." (RSV).

These two Beatitudes have not carried much weight in our culture, in America. In a number of locations around the world, the harsh reality of persecution is a difficult part of daily life. By and large, we have been spared that hardship. It seems those days are changing. I believe the further we go as a society, the more actual persecution we will see—and will be called on to face, manage appropriately, and endure.

What follows has nothing to do with politics and makes no political statement, reference, or inference. It is not a "proclamation," but more of a series of observations. It is not intended to be seen as a "doom and gloom" message, or one of criticism or judgment. On the contrary, it is a call to live in the presence of our Most High God, which is meant to be filled with his delight and glory and used to advance his Kingdom.

On election day in 2008, while working by myself in an empty house without any media source or any other input, around midday the Lord spoke the following to me and prompted me in further thought and dialogue with him, which went on for the rest of the day.

"Don't lament the loss. Work to win the lives. Work to gain the lives. America has made a decision today, the result of which will be continued and increased polarization. This only increases [the dynamics of] the spiritual climate, the need, the receptivity. This increase creates an environment that breeds insecurity, uncertainty, and fear. *I will be found there.* This environment develops, advances, the loss of a standard, of the standard, where many will move, will continue to move toward a human standard, to a 'standard' built on human 'wisdom.' Many others will search for something stronger, something of much higher value. *I will be found there.*"

He continued. "See it this way: 'Do not judge, lest you be judged,' and lose the opportunity. Do not argue, lest you harden the heart— yours and theirs—and lose the opportunity. Know and walk in this: 'And they overcame him because of the blood of the Lamb and because of the word of their testimony, and they did not love their life even [unto] death'" (Matthew 7:1; Revelation 12:11 NASB).

I was quite affected by this communiqué, to say the least. I spent the rest of the day listening and praying into this. What an opportunity with which we are presented!

The immediate context of Revelation 12:11 has all to do with spiritual warfare, with the actions of the accuser of the brethren. The application and the context also speak emphatically to our witness to those whom the Lord will draw to us.

Later that same day, in my time of intercession, he said, "Know and walk also in this: 'You are the salt of the earth; you are the light of the world. A city set on a hill cannot be hidden.'" This comes from Matthew 5:13–14. We are the salt; we are the light. He flavors and shines through us. Holy Spirit is the evangelist, the One who draws people to the salvation of the Christ. We are in partnership with him. This is where our focus, attention, and action must be. (This will be addressed further in chapter 12.)

He went on. "Consider a blister: The healing is in the wound. The fluid of a blister heals the damaged tissue." The Kingdom, the work of the Lord, among other things, is in the wound, is in the wounding, the darkness of the soul and also of the land. He is *found in the fear.* He is found in the pain, the wound. He will use the fall of man to draw mankind.

This prophetic word is the Father revealing the condition of the land, the truth about where it is headed, and the solution from within his heart. Consider the "spiritual polarization" and see within it the significant social and political divisions currently upon us.

There is more here. This prophetic word is also the Father revealing, perhaps exposing, the condition of the heart. There is a fear that develops within the soul when one moves toward God but does not fully yield. This is not fully engaging, connecting, and staying with him but rather being still somewhat in the world. It is being in a state of compromise. There is mixture in the soul. It is the tension found in being conflicted, part in and part out. Unfortunately, this is a fairly common occurrence in the Christian culture today; I dare say it is where most followers of Jesus find themselves living. It is not unlike September 12, 2001, the day after 9/11. That following Sunday, and for a short while afterward, the churches in America were full of people for any number of reasons, most not really connecting. That is not intended as a reflection on churches, good or bad. It is a reflection on the current condition of our human and societal nature. He requires us to be all in. We want our way. We want him our way; we truly are conflicted. He is more than willing to help us in this because he is constantly pursuing and drawing us to him. To live in this place of being in parts of two worlds is to be in the worst, most miserable place of occupancy possible. Galatians 5:16–17 spells this out quite clearly. "Live by the Spirit, and you will not gratify the desires of the sinful nature. For the sinful nature desires what is contrary to the Spirit, and the Spirit what is contrary to the sinful nature. They are in conflict with each other, so that you do not do what you want." It comes down to fighting the conviction of Holy Spirit with things that push him off—and also produce guilt and shame. It is wrestling against the conviction of the Lord, usually by distancing ourselves from him with more sin; it is an ugly, downward spiral. Certainly it is a tough spot to occupy. It's lukewarm, not fulfilled, and mostly dismal in either world.

O Father, O Jesus, help us. Help us to see this condition of our souls and to engage you and yield to you so we live where you want. Help us to capture fully your heart, these words from your heart, and engage them. We need you. We need your help. We need you to bring us ever closer to you so that we might walk with you, commune with you, and serve you. Deep does cry unto deep. Help us to hear the deep cry of your heart and respond fully.

[Selah]

On election day 2012, he fully reiterated this same word to me with the recognition that things had progressed further. Since then, usually around the first of the year, he has continued to expound on where things are and where they are going. In 2013 came the communiqué already discussed: "You are not ready. Get ready." In 2014 he said, "You are going to see unprecedented, unrestrained humanity." And we certainly have. In 2015 he stated, "It is no coincidence that you and yours are here in this time and place in history. You have been created for such a time as this." In 2016 the Lord said, "Waste and waste. I want you to waste, to spend yourself on me. Don't allow your life to be wasted. Don't allow your choices or the choices of others to waste your time, your energies, your life. You belong to me. Spend, waste yourself accordingly." In the early part of 2017 I had a series of visions that spoke to and indicated that considerable civil unrest was coming within my country, but also indicated the beginnings of a significant outpouring of the Spirit of God, with many new believers coming into his Kingdom. Surely the unrest has been present for some time now. It was the expression of the word *considerable* that stood out.

Then in 2018 came the communication to realize on one hand the continued moral decay in the land, the continued and proverbial unwillingness to admit the true condition of the heart, and the position many have taken to "cover over," or to "cover up," so as to ignore the wickedness, sin, and iniquity so prevalent. And, on the other hand, to recognize the extensiveness of the work he has done in the hearts of many in preparation, that it is time to engage, to align, with the seriousness of the call he has on the many who call on his name, and the impression to raise the level of being disciplined in him and enter into the fullness he has and is offering.

In further times of intercession, it became quite clear that all of the "you" and "your" mentions here are plural, that they are for all who call on the name of Jesus. Today, this series of communiqués from the Father surely rings true. It seems that things are continuing to accelerate.

In chapter 1 I said, "I am studying and writing on the Beatitudes for several reasons … To some extent, the timing for writing this book clearly has to do with the time in which we live." As a nation, we are experiencing increased anger and hatred in our land. There's a horrible increase of criticism and judgment in all forms of media, social and otherwise, that is producing a seemingly ever-increasing quantity of hate and hate crimes. We have become hypercritical and are seeing the amazing breakdown of all forms of respect, trust, and honor. There's a struggle with the continuing erosion of our constitution and the principles it represents, lending itself to lawlessness. The list goes on. There is a sometimes overwhelming fear in the hearts of so many, which exposes the certainly overwhelming need for the One and Only who can save us from all this, from ourselves. It appears that none of the above is going to slow down anytime soon.

The Word of God and his recently spoken prophetic words point to a sense, a knowing, that many will experience the brunt of all this. We are coming ever closer to a season of these things in our country. We must see that he is preparing us for this. We do well to see it coming, to pay attention to the warnings and the cautions. Be aware and be ready. Then there are no surprises. Then there will be no fear. Instead, there can be the peaceful, stable, secure, place found in Jesus wherein we can live, love, and react in a pure, merciful, true, and right manner.

Let's break down our passage: the more we know (epignosis), the wiser and safer we become. The Lord would have us to be "wise as serpents [that eye their opponents attentively[1]], and innocent as doves" (Matthew 10:16).

In verse 10 we find the phrase, "Bless-ed are those who are *persecuted*." This is one of those words, one of those hard realities reflected in the Word, that we all wish was not a part of our world. Yet it is. To persecute is "to pursue to the point of driving out." It is "to cause to suffer; to be [intentionally] mean to; to threaten [with intention to fulfill the threat]; to drive from place to place."[2] A clear example of this is when Saul, with the intent to kill, chased David around the countryside for years, with David hiding out in one cave after another (see the last third of 1 Samuel). To be persecuted is to "be chased, pursued, run after, driven away, all with hostile intentions." In our context, "persecution is caused by the world's hatred of God and his revelation in Christ." It is "hostility of the natural man against God and so also against the man, [the people,] led by God's Spirit."[3] This is seen in John 15:18 and following, where Jesus is preparing his disciples to understand and embrace what will be happening to them as he returns to his Father. He says in verse 18, "If the world hates you, keep in mind that it hated me first. If you belonged to the world, it would love you as its own. As it is, you do not belong to the world, but I have chosen you out of the world. That is why the world hates you."

It is true that messengers, the prophets of old, and the disciples from the days of Jesus until now have met and will meet with persecution (Matthew 5:11–12). "Hence persecution [is] a sign that one is on God's side, [thus the blessings of our verse]."[4] It is also true that we "are to meet the hatred of the persecutors with a word of blessing [and prayer and distinctly not lower ourselves to their level with a curse]"[5] (Matthew 5:44; Romans 12:14; paraphrase mine). And again, it is also true that "especially in persecution Christians experience the help, strength, and saving power of Christ; [when we are weak, then we are strong]"[6] (Romans 8:35–39; 2 Corinthians 4:8–9, 12:10b).

It is very necessary to understand that God does not bring persecution (or the insult, evil, and lying) we will see in the next verse. As "iron sharpens iron" (Proverbs 27:17), God can choose to use whatever humanity has brought forth to cause us to be challenged, for the purpose of growth. 1 Peter 2:20b says that in this we are to "suffer for doing good," and we are to "endure it, for this is commendable before God." It is how we mature in the Lord. In the context of the Beatitudes, this is to further tame us and bond us to him; it is the way to prautes. What is important to realize is that no matter what the source, at his discretion, God will use the circumstances and situations we find ourselves in to grow us. He is not the author of the persecution; he simply may or may not choose to use the challenge of it for our gain.

We are persecuted "because of righteousness." This is simply "the act of doing what God requires, what is right [according to him]."[7] It is this that stirs the hatred. We must understand that what is being defined and discussed for us by Jesus, what he is talking about, is being persecuted because we are living in a state of righteousness; we are in rightness with him, as defined by him. Although mostly not recognized, this stirs jealousy, tension, inner turmoil, and conviction in the hearts of those who are not born of the Spirit. The knowledge of God is in them, for God has made them so, but they are not yet willing to acknowledge it (Romans 1:19–20). I say *yet* because they may still say yes.

It is important to understand what is and what is not persecution so that it can be readily recognized when it does appear, and so we can righteously handle it. There are times when we are doubted, second-guessed, disagreed with, and discounted for our faith and for the position we have taken in Christ. That is not persecution. We may be the brunt of an argument against Jesus or Christianity, or religion, or the supernatural in general; that is also not persecution. Let's not overstate the situation but place the focus where it belongs, live in humble adoration of our King, and go from there.

In the beginnings of the Beatitudes (Matthew 5:3-12), in verse 3 it says, "Bless-ed are the poor in spirit, for theirs is the Kingdom of heaven." Then in verse 10 it says, "Bless-ed are those who are persecuted for righteousness' sake, for theirs is the Kingdom of heaven." The end of both verses is exactly the same. In Greek, this literary tool is called an *inclusio*. It is a technique used to bring inclusion or enclosure to all the communication between the two phrases. It is a way of tying it all together. As was said early on, the Beatitudes build upon one another. This inclusio brings literary, grammatical proof to that statement. The main purpose of an inclusio is to trigger the reader to recognize a significantly important message or theme is to be found between the phrases.

Back to the two verses. Expressed another way, bless-ed are those who are poor in spirit, due in part because of injustice, and bless-ed are those who are persecuted, due in part because of righteousness, the opposite of injustice. Both own the Kingdom of heaven. The word *own* is a present-tense verb; it is for now. If you are poor in spirit as we have come to understand it, and if you are experiencing persecution as we have come to understand it, then you own the Kingdom. Consider it this way: having faced and dealt with injustice, and so with justice, the reward is ownership of nothing less than God's Kingdom. The authorities, pleasures, and privileges of his Kingdom are yours. I'll take that! How about you?

"Bless-ed are you when people 'insult' you … and say all kinds of 'evil' against you 'falsely.'" To be offended or demeaned in this way is to be "spoken of in a very disparagingly manner."[8] When the consideration of *evil* is added to the mix, the words and their intention turn even darker, to a place of wickedness. The content of the speech "involves attributing evil to the person or persons,"[8] in this case to followers of Jesus. This is all accomplished by way of falsifying accounts and creating false statements against others. Unfortunately, there is already a considerable amount of this type of speech in our culture. It is not always aimed at Christians, but it certainly is gaining in quantity and intensity against those who call on the name of Jesus. Study history. As our culture continues to increase in humanism and the relativistic perspectives it perpetuates, the things of God will become more and more offensive to those who oppose them. As that continues to happen, the hatred toward believers in Jesus will grow. Do remember that the more this happens, the more bless-ed we are.

We come then to perhaps the key phrase within the entirety of the Beatitudes: "on account of me." This phrase is "a marker of cause," and it comes "with the implication of purpose."[9] It is a phrase that points the finger at the reason, the basis for all that surrounds it. From verses 10–12 and the challenges they reveal to the amazing character traits of the heart of Jesus found throughout the rest of the Beatitudes, this statement strongly illuminates the objective, intention, and purpose of it all. It is no coincidence that this phrase is placed as it is within the larger context. Jesus could have spoken it at any other point within the conversation, and it would have had merit. He chose to place it here for impact, for effect. It is as if he is emphatically saying,

"All of this, perhaps especially the difficulties that come with persecution and evil intent, are on account of me. If you will walk through life on account of me, you will come to and maintain victory on account of me."

All of this, from start to finish, is indeed on account of Jesus. In capturing this, it can be seen that the flow, and the sense therein, of this entire discourse now shifts and takes on a whole different genre. Now we see clearly the totality of these Beatitudes, these gracelets of glory, authored by the King of Glory. Now it all emerges and pours out as one overwhelming, intense, extremely poignant flurry of love and truth, from the heart of the One who is beyond all words and expressions to those he loves. There are no words …

From the next verse, which is verse 12, no wonder there's a call to "rejoice and be glad!" This phrase could be rendered as "rejoice and be glad" or "be glad and rejoice," as both words have very similar meanings. They are placed in purposeful redundancy to bring even more emphasis. In Greek, when two words of very similar meaning are used next to each other, it more than doubles the added meaning of each. This is a literary tool used to draw attention, to heighten awareness to what is being expressed. As well, this phrase is part of yet another inclusio. These two words are in the same semantic domain, the same family, as our word "bless-ed." These familial words, the first word of the Beatitudes, "bless-ed," and the last phrase, "rejoice and be glad," are wrapping themselves into and around the heart of the Beatitudes, around the beautifully expressed heart of God. When both of these literary tools are coupled thy cause a crescendo. It is literally, and literarily, bringing the orchestra of words to a climax beyond measure. Words bring expression. Here, these words have brought themselves beyond expression. It could be said that even the words, his words, have spent themselves on the Christ. Amazing.

Rejoice in this context is "to enjoy a state of extreme happiness and well-being."[10] To *be glad* is an "intensive joy and gladness, often implying verbal expression and body movement."[11] It is to shout and jump and dance with glee and great joy! The crescendo keeps rolling: the form of our phrase "be glad" is found nowhere else except here, not even in common, everyday Greek.[12] It is an expression exclusively for Jesus, to be shared with Jesus. It speaks to an energy, an excitement in the present that gets its essence and strength from a future event. It is the couple just engaged rejoicing and being glad for the wedding yet to come. For us, this is reflective of, and has all to do with, the rewards of heaven experienced in part here and now. Hallelujah!

When we have encircled, apprehended, and embarked on all that is herein, then we are full-on ready for and engaged in the day in which we live.

Chapter 12

Salt and Light

Matthew 5:13–16 states,

> You are the salt of the earth. But if the salt loses its saltiness, how can it be made salty again? It is no longer good for anything, except to be thrown out and trampled by men. You are the light of the world. A city on a hill cannot be hidden. Neither do people light a lamp and put it under a bowl. Instead they put it on its stand, and it gives light to everyone in the house. In the same way, let your light shine before men, that they may see your good deeds and praise your Father in heaven.

We come now to the end of our journey. I hope it has been as enjoyable for you as it has been for me. I hope and pray that you have met with Jesus within the pages of this book, at a deeper and richer level than ever before.

I have included these verses that talk about salt and light in this book for several reasons. Literarily and grammatically, by way of content and intent, they flow with the previous ten verses. They comprise a closing or concluding statement. They also provide a very strong assignment. I am not saying they do not belong as presented. I am saying they are attached, and they involve an overlap in structure and substance. They belong.

Salt and light are both basic elements and components of life; they are vital to our existence. Jesus is using something vital to speak something vital. You are the salt of the earth; you are the light of the world. These two verses are quite potent. They are emphatic, which means they are pointed and direct and carry weight. They are not suggestions; each is a fact and then a command. Both are written in such a manner as to deliver a distinct, poignant, heart-and-soul-affecting message. They are aimed at those who know and walk with Jesus. He is speaking to his disciples, then and now. Having poured his heart out proclaiming the fullness that we find in his Beatitudes, he is now bringing home the final application. Certainly, there are applications in his teachings all throughout; it all comes home here. We have gone from first to last.

As has become our custom, let's break these verses down a bit.

In Greek, the *you* is actually "you, yourself," which is always a way of bringing intensity to the word and getting the recipient's attention. It might be as though, if you and Jesus were standing face-to-face with each other, and he was speaking these statements to you, he would be sure you were looking him in the eye while he had his hands on your shoulders to gain your full focus and attention. "You are the salt of the earth; you are the light of the world!" In light of the potency here, this statement could be expanded and read as, "I am with you always, yes. You need to understand it is on you to be salt and light. It is on you to model salt and light. It is on you to express, to manifest salt and light in the world around you. As my disciples, this is your assignment." Said another way, "If you are walking with me as I have outlined and explained here, you are my disciples; now go make some." A German scholar in the early 1960s studied this passage and said, "Flavorless salt and a covered lamp are alike useless; so the disciple of Christ who fails to be stimulating and bright in the work that God wants done is good for nothing."[1] Okay, then. That might be a bit harsh, but the point is well identified! Here it is: With the Beatitudes having fully and thoroughly laid out the outline and details of living life on this planet the way that Jesus wants and requires, having laid his heart bare in offering this to us as the ways and means to life, and having later laid it not just bare but down on the Cross, he is commanding us to follow his directives to the full. The intensity of his love and his purpose for us is directly reflected in these commands. This intensity is expressed here, throughout his time on earth, and at the end of his time on earth in the Great Commandment: "Go! Make disciples! I will be with you forever!" (Matthew 28:18–20; paraphrase mine).

Making disciples is the call. It is not the only one, but it is one of the primary and natural results, natural conclusions, of these Beatitudes. It needs to seen for what it is. Jesus is not asking us to muster up some energy and go save the world. That is not who he is or how he works. Because all things in his Kingdom are based on and revolve around relationships, it is within that context that evangelism and discipleship take place. For example, I share Jesus with others not from guilt or compulsion, but from the surplus of him in my heart. That is all he is asking for from any of us. If you don't have that surplus, get some! That is your job. If my wife is in Chicago and I'm not, and I want some time with her, I can either sit around and grumble about what isn't, or I can figure out a way to get to Chicago. That is up to me! Our job in our relationship with God is to position ourselves to receive. It is that simple. He first loved us (1 John 4:19), he is in constant pursuit of us (John 3:16–17, 15:5, 9), and he is asking for us to pursue him back (Matthew 6:33). Let's figure that out and go there.

A few years back, it became necessary to spend some time at my parental home along with two of my sisters. Dad could no longer take care of himself and needed full-time assistance. We three took on that home to remove all the contents to prepare it for sale. There were sixty-plus years' worth of memories and connected paraphernalia to sort through, relive, and scrutinize so as to determine their next location. It took us three days and who knows how many laughs and cries. At one point, I was over by the furnace, and I came upon the wood box, a place where scrap pieces of wood had been stored in case they were needed. Nothing ever got thrown away in that home! I came across a piece of wood that stopped me in my tracks and broke me. It was a four by six about two feet long. There must have been at least a hundred nails in it—shingle nails, I expect, because they had a larger head and were easier to hit with a hammer than a common nail. I remembered it well then, and I remember it the same today. I'd done that. I'd pounded those nails in that block of wood. Dad was at the workbench pounding some nails into something to repair it, and I just wanted to be with him and do what he was doing. He set me up to pound away and get me out of his hair for a few hours. I was a simple, innocent little boy looking for love, looking for relationship with the one who, by nature, was the most important one to me. For me, there was no agenda, there were no parameters, and there were not even any rules; it was simply the undefined, deep need and cry in my heart to be loved. God put that love in there. He put it in all of us, all 7.5 billion of us. He created that love. He took it from his heart and placed it in mine, without reserve and without reservation. Pure, unalloyed, undiluted, filled-with-compassion-and-care love.

All these years later, I can say that the dad-son relationship thing did not work out too well. But in the midst of all that that statement entails, I can also say that the Father-son relationship more than makes up for what the other one was lacking. That is not testimony to my dad; he did the best he knew to do within his own struggles and pain. That is testimony to my heavenly Father. And here it is: with my dad, I could pound those nails and connect it in my mind that I helped fix that broken chair. It is honestly not much different with our heavenly Father. Little Sammy helps build the new shed by pounding those same few nails while dad works away to get it built. Then when it's done, he goes and brags to Mommy about the shed he built! We do that same thing with the Father, and he does that same thing with us! He sets us up for love, for life, and for the sense of value and purpose that we gain working with him. We pound a few nails and get fulfilled because he set it up that way. Dad does not need Sammy to accomplish the task. Sammy needs dad. Only with our Creator Father, the transactions between us that so affect the heart are right and pure and whole. And when it is all over, we are made whole.

As has been previously stated, the Father wants none to perish, but for all to come to him and enter into relationship with him now and for eternity (2 Peter 3:9). He does not have to, but he wants to use us to bring that about. We are the salt. We are the light. When we love and follow Jesus, we reflect him. From there, we flavor and illuminate the world around us. If we will yield and consent, he will love us, he will use us, and he will flow through us to bring those currently lost to him. We just pound a few nails, while in love he works away to get it done.

You are the salt of the earth. You are the light of the world. Our words here are very basic; they mostly mean what they say, with a few nuances. *Salt* in this context is natural salt, one of Earth's basic minerals, which came from several different sources. This fact determined the purity, and thus the value, of the salt. It was used to flavor, enhance, enlighten, or enrich. It was also used as a preservative so as to protect from harm and promote the healing process. As salt was so much a part of everyday life and had a variety of uses, the word became woven into everyday language in an assortment of ways. For example, "to 'eat someone's salt', or 'to eat the proverbial salt' was to be on friendly terms with [that person]; it was to enjoy [their] hospitality." Also, "to 'have eaten a bushel of salt together' was to be old friends." And then, "to 'eat the salt of the palace' was to express loyalty in the relationship of employee to employer."[2]

There are several Greek words that translate into English as *light*. This particular word is interesting in that it is "light that is never kindled and therefore never quenched."[3] To never be kindled is to never have been started or ignited from fire or the like, so it can never be extinguished. It is like light from the sun or a star. The "original, literal meaning" of this word supports this, as it "is found in reference to the sun."[4] When Jesus is saying this in reference to his disciples, he is labeling them as unquenchable. We are his disciples today, and it is the same label. As the lamp in the text is referring to a common, everyday oil lamp, which is kindled, it is easy to assume that the light Jesus is referencing is the same. However, the focal point of his communication is not that the lamp can be extinguished but that it can be covered. The fact that Jesus chose to use the word he did speaks volumes; he could have picked a different word to illustrate what he was talking about.

I believe it is the second half of these verses that is actually the most important for us to consider. The first sentence in each verse makes a clear statement that is self-contained and stands alone, and the heart of Jesus is evident, strong, and certain. The second parts address the humanity within those identified as disciples and allude to our potential weaknesses and struggles. From our text: "But if the salt 'loses its saltiness', how can it be made salty again?" and "Neither do people light a lamp and 'put it under a bowl.'" Let's examine.

Much of the salt mined from the ground was impure and would, in fact, lose its saltiness over time. This was due to several factors involved in the mining process. Dirt, dust, particles of gypsum that were found mixed with the salt—all of these contributed to impurity. This salt, thus spent, would lose its saltiness and be thrown out. Often it was used to fill potholes in the roadways or on residential rooftops that were used by the family living there. Thus, "to be thrown out and trampled by men." The phrase "lose its saltiness" literally translates to "I am foolish,"[5] as seen also in Romans 1:22, "they became fools." It was a common phrase that meant "to become or make foolish," "to make dull," or "to cause something to lose the purpose for which it exists."[6] Bringing that to bear in our world, if we lose our saltiness, we lose our purpose. Ouch! Unfortunately, in our culture at large, we have done just that more often than not. I don't say that by way of a criticism or a judgment, only as an observation. What an opportunity we now have to regain.

At some point in time, the question must be asked and answered: Why are you here? It is such a very basic question, and yet in our day and age, many do not know the answer. Many more are not knowingly asking; they do not even know to ask. It is fairly easy to answer this question negatively; it is easy to point out what the answer is not. You are not here to work too hard, retire too late, and die. You are not here to just raise a family. You are not here to build a business or invent the latest thingamajig! You are not here to impress others or to live your life focused on how wonderful or smart or beautiful you are. Although all of these things have merit and value, generally and specifically in God's economy, none of them answers the question.

Why are you here, on this planet and at this time in history? I spent over twenty years in a particular industry as a diagnostician, a troubleshooter, solving other people's problems. I would not have lasted a year except for this: I learned to ask the right questions. By doing that, I was well on my way to finding the right answer and bringing a solution to the problem. The right answer usually comes from the one who knows, from the one who was in on the creation of the thing in the first place. In this context, that would be God. That having been identified, I don't suggest asking God why you are here. My experience with him offers two thoughts on that: (1) He almost never answers the "Why?" question. (2) He almost never answers a question that he has already answered. It's in the Book! Here is my answer:

In the beginning, God created the heavens and the earth, all for the purposes of relationship. Then Father, Son, and Holy Spirit created mankind in their image—their shadow, actually—all for the purposes of relationship then, now, and forever. They gave the earth to their creation, to us humans. After we fumbled it away (and our souls with it), Jesus came and took it all back—and gave it to us again, with him in the mix this time, all for the purposes of relationship. On the other side of this bubble we call time, on the other side of this story, there is a wedding complete with a feast around a banqueting table, all for the purposes of relationship. There the bridegroom will embrace, delightfully capture and marry his bride, and off into eternity they will go. It is the most amazing love scene in all of time and history, and truthfully in all of eternity. The angels can hardly wait! It is the only scene in the entirety of scenes, in all of time, that truly ends with them living happily ever after. All other similar scenes are just a novel, a movie, or a theatrical performance; they're not really real. Why is this all true and real? One more time: it's all for the purposes of relationship. We have been created to worship God in spirit and in truth, which is from the core of our souls, and to share his love and good news with others so they can do the same. All of the other things we do or are a part of have value, yes. But none of them are the reason; they are simply a means to an end, his means to his purposes and intentions.

Please capture this: All that the Creator of the Universe, the Almighty God of Heaven and Earth, the Pursuer and the Lover of your soul, has ever wanted and has ever accomplished from beginning to end, he has done from a place of love, from a place of desire for relationship with those he loves. His heart's desire is simply that and nothing more. He is passionately and overwhelmingly in love with his creation, with you and me. I started this book with this truth, and I will end it here the same. Why did God create the Earth? For you. Why did he establish people, you and me, on his Earth? Because of his capacity for and desire to love. Because he wanted a bride for his Son. Because he wanted a love relationship that was true, deep, and rich for his Son, and from there for himself. You take his breath away, you overwhelm him, and he cannot stop himself. He created and built it all for you. He is all in for you forever, but not just for you. He's for all of the yous on the planet. Had there been just one you, he would have done it the same. But he wants all the yous. That brings us right back to salt and light.

Pure salt, sodium chloride, is a very stable compound and does not readily breakdown. There is a question, based on the chemistry of it, regarding whether it is even possible for sodium chloride to disintegrate or degenerate to that place of no longer being classified as salt, being no longer salty. I have a very good friend who is a Doctor of Chiropractic with undergrad degrees in biology and chemistry. I interviewed her on this subject matter, asking three questions: (1) Can salt actually lose its saltiness? (2) If so, how? (3) If so, can it regain its saltiness? Her answers are quite revelatory in our context. Yes, under the right circumstances, salt can indeed lose its saltiness. This can happen in three different manners. It can happen by dilution, by oxidation, or by being inappropriately exposed to the elements around it. One can readily see where this is going. If we are the salt, we can lose our saltiness by being so diluted, so watered down by the world, the devil, and our flesh, that we no longer are salty. This has all to do with the choices we make, with to whom and to what we say yes. If we are the salt, we can lose our saltiness by oxidation, which in the world of ferrous metals is rust, and which in the world of human health is cancer. This happens by lack of use, or improper use, or lack of intention. This also has all to do with the choices we make. For example, if I choose to disengage from the people and the world around me; if I intentionally decide to succumb to the temptation to isolate, to ignore, to stick my head in the sand and pay no attention to my surroundings and how they affect me; I will rust, I will oxidize, and I will lose my saltiness. If we are the salt and live in this manner, we are being inappropriately exposed to the elements around us, and we lose.

That brings us to my third question: Can salt regain its saltiness? In the natural realm, the answer is an emphatic no. It is not chemically possible that once sodium chloride has been broken down, it can be restored. But we are not sodium chloride! We are men and women with hearts and souls; we are complex creatures with many moving parts. By the grace and mercy of the Lord Jesus, the Christ, and our Abba Father, we can be fully and completely restored. We have been redeemed, purchased by the shed blood of Jesus, which means we are not our own but are owned by him.

He has the ability and the desire to restore; he is in the restoration business. He awaits our asking. This truth is seen also in the fact that as light, we are unable to be extinguished. We can be covered, and we can cover ourselves in the same manner that we become unsalty, but God is still God in any and all situations. He is the God of the 2nd chance, and the 22nd chance, and even the 222nd chance if he needs to be.

Yes, we are salt and light. Yes, we are thus anointed, commissioned, and empowered. See that salt can lose its saltiness and light can be covered. See that with God, all things are possible. Settle into prautes and all it entails. Settle into mourning, hungering, and thirsting for righteousness and justice, as well as the action that is found there. Settle into mercy, peace, and purity, and you will become merciful, peaceful, and pure. That is salt and light! Rise to the occasion. Go "eat someone's salt." You have now been exposed to the depth of the heart of Jesus and his Father. You have been encouraged and challenged to enter in. The only thing standing in your way is you, your hesitancy, your fear. Perfect love casts out fear (1 John 4:18). Love's name is Jesus, so if you are aligned with him, there is nothing left to fear. Run toward the roar. Walk to and through the fear and all its complexities; Jesus is here to help you. Get outside your self. Reach out. Invest in others. Develop relationships so you too can say you have "eaten a bushel of salt together." Let Jesus flow into and then through you and watch and see what he will do!

We believers have an opportunity in front of us that may very well prove to be the most powerful and important opportunity in the history of man. That is a huge statement. I believe if you will listen, if you will seek and hear what the Lord is saying in the earth, you will recognize the truth in it. Bless-ed are you; favored, honored, and highly esteemed are you. Walk fully in these Beatitudes, these principles for life. "Let your light shine [and your salt be salty!] before men, that they may see your good deeds and praise your Father in heaven." Walk fully in the grace, power, and presence of the Lord and Savior Jesus, the Christ. Walk in, walk with, walk on with Him. See the opportunity; seize the opportunity. Go forth, you "awful thing"!

Endnotes

Introduction

1 *The New Strong's Exhaustive Concordance of the Bible*. Nashville, TN: Thomas Nelson Publishers, 1990.
2 Genesis 15:6; Romans 4:11–12; James 2:21.
3 *The New Strong's Exhaustive Concordance of the Bible*. Nashville, TN: Thomas Nelson Publishers, 1990.
4 Guralnik, David B. *New World Dictionary, Second College Edition*. Cleveland, OH: William Collins Publishers, Inc., 1979.

Chapter 1

1 Brown, Colin. *The New International Dictionary of New Testament Theology* (NIDNTT). Grand Rapids, MI: Zondervan Publishing House, 1986.
2 Jones, Alanzo T. *Studies in the Book of Galatians*. Fort Oglethorpe, GA: Teach Services, Inc., 2002.
3 From my journal. In the midst of some intense prayer and worship time, as I was pouring out my heart to the Lord regarding a deep challenge in my heart, from his heart of love, he responded to me, "Stay close, son. We will work through this together." And we have.

4 Barker, Kenneth. *The NIV Study Bible,* Study Notes. Grand Rapids, MI: Zondervan Bible Publishers, 1985.
5 *The New Strong's Exhaustive Concordance of the Bible.* Nashville, TN: Thomas Nelson Publishers, 1990.
6 Brown, Colin. *The New International Dictionary of New Testament Theology* (NIDNTT), Grand Rapids, MI: Zondervan Publishing House, 1986.
7 Ladd, George Eldon. A *Theology of the New Testament.* Grand Rapids, MI: William B. Eerdmans Publishing Company, 1996.

Chapter 2

1 Isaiah 62:1–5; John 3:27–29; Matthew 9:15; 2 Corinthians 11:2; Revelation 19:7, 21:9, 22:17. These Scriptures, and others that are connected, clearly reveal the heart and intent of the Father regarding his ongoing plan for and with his creation.
2 Barker, Kenneth. *The NIV Study Bible,* Study Notes. Grand Rapids, MI: Zondervan Bible Publishers, 1985.
3 Brown, Colin. *The New International Dictionary of New Testament Theology* (NIDNTT). Grand Rapids, MI: Zondervan Publishing House, 1986.
4 Zodhiates, Spiros. *The Complete Word Study Dictionary, New Testament.* Chattanooga, TN: AMG Publishers, 1992.
5 Ibid.
6 Ibid.
7 Ibid.
8 Ibid.

Chapter 3

1 Louw, Johannes, and Eugene Nida. *Greek-English Lexicon of the New Testament.* New York, NY: United Bible Societies, 1989.
2 Guralnik, David B. *New World Dictionary, Second College Edition.* Cleveland, OH: William Collins Publishers, Inc., 1979.
3 Kolhenberger III, John R. *The Expanded Vine's Expository Dictionary of New Testament Words.* Minneapolis, MN: Bethany House Publishers, 1984.
4 Louw, Johannes, and Eugene Nida. *Greek-English Lexicon of the New Testament.* New York, NY: United Bible Societies, 1989.

5 Kittel, Gerhard, and Gerhard Friedrich. *Theological Dictionary of the New Testament* (TDNT). Grand Rapids, MI: William B. Eerdmans Publishing Company, 1968.
6 Zodhiates, Spiros. *The Complete Word Study Dictionary, New Testament.* Chattanooga, TN: AMG Publishers, 1992.
7 White, Ron. *The Blue Collar Comedy Tour.* 2007.
8 *The New Strong's Exhaustive Concordance of the Bible.* Nashville, TN: Thomas Nelson Publishers, 1990.
9 Louw, Johannes, and Eugene Nida. *Greek-English Lexicon of the New Testament.* New York, NY: United Bible Societies, 1989.
10 Brown, Colin. *The New International Dictionary of New Testament Theology* (NIDNTT). Grand Rapids, MI: Zondervan Publishing House, 1986.

Chapter 4

1 *The New Strong's Exhaustive Concordance of the Bible.* Nashville, TN: Thomas Nelson Publishers, 1990.
2 Louw, Johannes, and Eugene Nida. *Greek-English Lexicon of the New Testament.* New York, NY: United Bible Societies, 1989.
3 Rogers, Jr., Cleon L. and Cleon L. Rogers III. *The New Linguistic and Exegetical Key to the Greek New Testament.* Grand Rapids, MI: Zondervan Publishing House, 1998.
4 Kittel, Gerhard, and Gerhard Friedrich. *Theological Dictionary of the New Testament* (TDNT). Grand Rapids, MI: William B. Eerdmans Publishing Company, 1968.
5 Ibid.
6 Louw, Johannes, and Eugene Nida. *Greek-English Lexicon of the New Testament.* New York, NY: United Bible Societies, 1989.
7 Kittel, Gerhard, and Gerhard Friedrich. *Theological Dictionary of the New Testament* (TDNT). Grand Rapids, MI: William B. Eerdmans Publishing Company, 1968.
8 Bromiley, Geoffery W. *The International Standard Bible Encyclopedia* (ISBE). Grand Rapids, MI: William B. Eerdmans Publishing Company, 1986. These words mean "beating the breast," "be dark," or "dirty from being in mourning attire (from rolling in the dirt)," and "a type of musical composition, a dirge," respectively.
9 Guralnik, David B. *New World Dictionary, Second College Edition.* Cleveland, OH: William Collins Publishers, Inc., 1979.

10 *The New Strong's Exhaustive Concordance of the Bible*. Nashville, TN: Thomas Nelson Publishers, 1990.

11 Louw, Johannes, and Eugene Nida. *Greek-English Lexicon of the New Testament*. New York, NY: United Bible Societies, 1989.

12 *The New Strong's Exhaustive Concordance of the Bible*. Nashville, TN: Thomas Nelson Publishers, 1990.

13 Cairns, Alan. *Dictionary of Theological Terms*. Greenville, SC: Emerald House Group, Inc., 1998.

14 Guralnik, David B. *New World Dictionary, Second College Edition*. Cleveland, OH: William Collins Publishers, Inc., 1979.

15 Once, under the direction of the Lord, I created, owned, and operated a carpet-cleaning company. It is very hard and often very hot work. Heavy physical work among 210-degree water tends to make one quite hot—and quite exhausted by day's end. On one particularly hot afternoon, I finished a job and was tearing down equipment and loading up the truck. Part of that process was disconnecting the water supply: a garden hose connected to the house in which I was working. There was always water pressure on the hose, so disconnecting it was a bit tricky. On this day, as I was disconnecting the coupler, my elbow was bumped, and I received a significant amount of cold water squarely in my face! Immediately I heard the voice of the Lord laughing. I felt the bump. He had bumped my elbow, at just the right moment, to make the coupler jostle in just the right way and spray water in my face. He was having some fun with me. It was quite refreshing! I was blessed, both physically with the cold water and relationally with his presence impacting me in such a fun manner.

Chapter 5

1 Guralnik, David B. *New World Dictionary, Second College Edition*. Cleveland, OH: William Collins Publishers, Inc., 1979.

2 Kittel, Gerhard, Gerhard Friedrich. *Theological Dictionary of the New Testament* (TDNT). Grand Rapids, MI: William B. Eerdmans Publishing Company, 1968.

3 Zodhiates, Spiros. *The Complete Word Study Dictionary, New Testament*. Chattanooga, TN: AMG Publishers, 1992.

4 Harris, Laird R., Gleason L. Archer, Jr., and Bruce K. Waltke. *Theological Wordbook of the Old Testament* (TWOT). Chicago, IL: Moody Press, 1980.

5 Brown, Colin. *The New International Dictionary of New Testament Theology* (NIDNTT). Grand Rapids, MI: Zondervan Publishing House, 1986.
6 Kittel, Gerhard, and Gerhard Friedrich. *Theological Dictionary of the New Testament* (TDNT). Grand Rapids, MI: William B. Eerdmans Publishing Company, 1968.
7 Zodhiates, Spiros. *The Complete Word Study Dictionary, New Testament.* Chattanooga, TN: AMG Publishers, 1992.
8 Kittel, Gerhard, and Gerhard Friedrich. *Theological Dictionary of the New Testament* (TDNT). Grand Rapids, MI: William B. Eerdmans Publishing Company, 1968.
9 Ibid.
10 Ibid.
11 Kolhenberger III, John R. *The Expanded Vine's Expository Dictionary of New Testament Words.* Minneapolis, MN: Bethany House Publishers, 1984.
12 Ibid.

Chapter 6

1 Source unknown.
2 Source unknown.

Chapter 7

1 Kittel, Gerhard, and Gerhard Friedrich. *Theological Dictionary of the New Testament* (TDNT). Grand Rapids, MI: William B. Eerdmans Publishing Company, 1968.
2 *The New Strong's Exhaustive Concordance of the Bible.* Nashville, TN: Thomas Nelson Publishers, 1990.
3 Brown, Colin. *The New International Dictionary of New Testament Theology* (NIDNTT). Grand Rapids, MI: Zondervan Publishing House, 1986.
4 Kittel, Gerhard, and Gerhard Friedrich. *Theological Dictionary of the New Testament* (TDNT). Grand Rapids, MI: William B. Eerdmans Publishing Company, 1968.
5 Hagner, Donald A. *Word Biblical Commentary, Volume* 33A. Dallas, TX: Word Books, 1993.
6 Brown, Colin. *The New International Dictionary of New Testament Theology* (NIDNTT). Grand Rapids, MI: Zondervan Publishing House, 1986.

7 Louw, Johannes, and Eugene Nida. *Greek-English Lexicon of the New Testament.* New York, NY: United Bible Societies, 1989.
8 Ibid.
9 Kittel, Gerhard, and Gerhard Friedrich. *Theological Dictionary of the New Testament* (TDNT). Grand Rapids, MI: William B. Eerdmans Publishing Company, 1968.
10 Brown, Colin. *The New International Dictionary of New Testament Theology* (NIDNTT). Grand Rapids, MI: Zondervan Publishing House, 1986.
11 Kittel, Gerhard, and Gerhard Friedrich. *Theological Dictionary of the New Testament* (TDNT). Grand Rapids, MI: William B. Eerdmans Publishing Company, 1968.

Chapter 8

1 Hagner, Donald A. *Word Biblical Commentary, Volume* 33A. Dallas, TX: Word Books, 1993.
2 Brown, Colin. *The New International Dictionary of New Testament Theology* (NIDNTT). Grand Rapids, MI: Zondervan Publishing House, 1986.
3 Louw, Johannes, and Eugene Nida. *Greek-English Lexicon of the New Testament.* New York, NY: United Bible Societies, 1989.

Chapter 9

1 Brown, Colin. *The New International Dictionary of New Testament Theology* (NIDNTT). Grand Rapids, MI: Zondervan Publishing House, 1986.
2 Ibid.
3 Zodhiates, Spiros. *The Complete Word Study Dictionary, New Testament.* Chattanooga, TN: AMG Publishers, 1992.
4 Brown, Colin. *The New International Dictionary of New Testament Theology* (NIDNTT). Grand Rapids, MI: Zondervan Publishing House, 1986.
5 *The New Strong's Exhaustive Concordance of the Bible.* Nashville, TN: Thomas Nelson Publishers, 1990.
6 Zodhiates, Spiros. *The Complete Word Study Dictionary, New Testament.* Chattanooga, TN: AMG Publishers, 1992.
7 Goodrick, Edward W., and John R. Kohlenberger III. *Zondervan NIV Exhaustive Concordance.* Grand Rapids, MI: Zondervan Publishing House 1999.

8 Guralnik, David B. *New World Dictionary, Second College Edition.*, Cleveland, OH: William Collins Publishers, Inc., 1979.
9 *The New Strong's Exhaustive Concordance of the Bible.* Nashville, TN: Thomas Nelson Publishers, 1990.
10 Louw, Johannes, and Nida, Eugene. *Greek-English Lexicon of the New Testament.* New York, NY: United Bible Societies, 1989.
11 Ibid.
12 Ibid.
13 Ibid.
14 Ibid.
15 Brown, Colin. *The New International Dictionary of New Testament Theology* (NIDNTT). Grand Rapids, MI: Zondervan Publishing House, 1986.
16 Van Gemeren, William A. *New International Dictionary of Old Testament Theology & Exegesis* (NIDOTTE). Wheaton, IL: Tyndale House Publishers, 1999.
17 Louw, Johannes, and Eugene Nida. *Greek-English Lexicon of the New Testament.* New York, NY: United Bible Societies, 1989.

Chapter 10

1 Brown, Colin. *The New International Dictionary of New Testament Theology* (NIDNTT). Grand Rapids, MI: Zondervan Publishing House, 1986.
2 Ibid.
3 Chambers, Oswald. *My Utmost for His Highest.* New York, NY: Dodd, Mead & Company, 1935.
4 The word *shema*, which is from Deuteronomy 6:4 and following, is often referred to as "The Shema," and is a great study on relationship and priorities with the Lord within his economy, his Kingdom.
5 Seekins, Dr. Frank T. *Hebrew Word Pictures.* Phoenix, AZ: Living Word Pictures, Inc., 2003.
6 *The New Strong's Exhaustive Concordance of the Bible.* Nashville, TN: Thomas Nelson Publishers, 1990.
7 Zodhiates, Spiros. *The Complete Word Study Dictionary, New Testament.* Chattanooga, TN: AMG Publishers, 1992.
8 *The New Strong's Exhaustive Concordance of the Bible.* Nashville, TN: Thomas Nelson Publishers, 1990.

9 Guralnik, David B. *New World Dictionary, Second College Edition.* Cleveland, OH: William Collins Publishers, Inc., 1979.

Chapter 11

1 Zodhiates, Spiros. *The Complete Word Study Dictionary, New Testament.* Chattanooga, TN: AMG Publishers, 1992.
2 Louw, Johannes, and Eugene Nida. *Greek-English Lexicon of the New Testament.* New York, NY: United Bible Societies, 1989.
3 Brown, Colin. *The New International Dictionary of New Testament Theology* (NIDNTT). Grand Rapids, MI: Zondervan Publishing House, 1986.
4 Ibid.
5 Ibid.
6 Ibid.
7 Louw, Johannes, and Eugene Nida. *Greek-English Lexicon of the New Testament.* New York, NY: United Bible Societies, 1989.
8 Ibid.
9 Ibid.
10 Ibid.
11 Ibid.
12 Brown, Colin. *The New International Dictionary of New Testament Theology* (NIDNTT). Grand Rapids, MI: Zondervan Publishing House, 1986.

Chapter 12

1 Brown, Colin. *The New International Dictionary of New Testament Theology* (NIDNTT). Grand Rapids, MI: Zondervan Publishing House, 1986.
2 Ibid.
3 Zodhiates, Spiros. *The Complete Word Study Dictionary, New Testament.* Chattanooga, TN: AMG Publishers, 1992.
4 Brown, Colin. *The New International Dictionary of New Testament Theology* (NIDNTT). Grand Rapids, MI: Zondervan Publishing House, 1986.
5 McReynolds, Paul R. *Word Study Greek-English New Testament.* Wheaton, IL: Tyndale House Publishers, Inc., 1999.
6 Source unknown.

Printed in the United States
By Bookmasters